Marilyn,

Enjoy your today but love your tomorrow.

A Father
A Son
and A House
Full of Ghosts

BOOK TWO

Gregory Young

ISBN 0-7414-4218-3

Published by:

PUBLISHING.COM

1094 New DeHaven Street, Suite 100
West Conshohocken, PA 19428-2713
Info@buybooksontheweb.com
www.buybooksontheweb.com
Toll-free (877) BUY BOOK
Local Phone (610) 941-9999
Fax (610) 941-9959

Printed in the United States of America

Printed on Recycled Paper

Published October 2007

The names in this story are actual, the dialogue is real, and the stories are true.

Special Thanks To:

Sharon Dvorak and Joseph Young

Thank You For Your Stories:

Gregory Adams, Judith DeBrosse, Martha Cella, Kathy Davis, Tara Decamillo, Theresa Einhaus, Luisa Dinis Ferrer, A.H., Lynn Jenkins, Teresa Jones, Lilli Marchiani, Sabina Muller, D.M., Greta Pacevich, S. and J. Poloff, Maria Schumann, Kathy Shivers, J.S., Diana Sweeney, Dolores Clark Talbot, Jane, Abigail, Alec Ward, Stacy Young

CONTENTS:

INTRODUCTION

Much is heard but not so much seen. In short, this house has me very tense. I have become very much on edge living here. I know that I said in the last book that I wasn't afraid of the things going on, but lately I'm nervous and many times, have been scared.

I'm always hearing things. I've woken up in the middle of the night to bats flying around my bedroom. I see waves of movement rippling throughout different rooms. I witnessed a cloud of light misty haze move across the living room air.

The pictures of orbs are bigger and clearer. I feel tugging on my shirt and then there was that voice that called my name in the middle of my sleep.

Sometimes, I'm awakened by sounds of...I don't even know what. Sounds that can't be identified. I wake up in a panic. I jolt up from my bed short of breath gasping for air looking around the room for something to be there.

"Jonathan, Sarah? Is that you?

There is never a response.

I haven't been sleeping. My eyes open at the slightest sound of noise or at anything that may look like movement around the bedroom.

Sometimes I'll stay up as long as I can downstairs just so that when I do go to bed I'll fall asleep quickly.

I know that they are listening to me. I know they are watching me, and I know they have communicated with me. It is up to me to pay attention to it.

It's not so much lights going off and on now or things appearing or disappearing like it used to be. Things have changed, they're a bit different now, almost as if they have risen to a new level.

And it's not so much for me to be afraid of, it's more of just a matter of shock. I never know what is going to happen next or when.

Many people have called my house haunted. That's okay with me if that's how they want to see it. I don't see it that way. The spirits living here are friendly. They are not monsters or creatures of the night or anything that would be considered fear based. They are at peace and simply have a desire to have their presence known.

I see this experience as a gift that has been given to me. Not many people get the chance to have what I have in my home, and to experience the experience. And for now, I'd much rather deal with the shock, the surprises and the unexpected than to not have it at all. It is rare and I know not to take it for granted.

I'm not going to ask them to leave. They can stay as long as they would like to. I will continue to talk to them, invite them to go places with me and I will ask for their help if I feel I need it.

In this house they consider me part of their family and it only feels natural for me to consider them part of mine.

ELIZABETH AGNES JENSEN

1820-1898

The older woman living here with my son and I has the name Elizabeth Agnes Jensen. She was born January 3rd 1820 and died at seventy-eight years old in 1898.

She prefers that we call her by her middle name –Agnes. As a human, and having the name of Elizabeth, she was often called "Lizzy" and she did not like that. Therefore, she asks that we refer to her as Agnes.

She has been with me for fourteen years. Agnes was drawn to me from spirit because I very much reminded her of herself and of a man that she knew who had proposed to her. She did not accept the proposal.

Agnes did marry at fourteen years old, and her husband worked in the newspaper business. They lived in the United States, in the area we now know as Chicago, and they had one son named Edward.

Agnes was seventeen years old at the beginning of the Victorian era in 1837, and had already been married for three years.

She remembers enjoying the clothing of that era. She very much enjoyed all of the hats, the lace, ribbons and pleating. She also had a great appreciation for the very fine needle work. She enjoyed dressing for special occasions when she was able to be dressed as she says, "like a peacock," but complained that the shoes were too tight for her. They were designed and created to be very narrow which often hurt her feet.

In Agnes' spare time she enjoyed writing, singing, needle point and baking, particularly the baking of breads.

She found great satisfaction in helping others who were sick or unable to care for themselves and she enjoyed assisting them in their time of need.

She became a widow at fifty-one and eventually had a woman come to live with her who would help her around her home. But most of Agnes' later years were lonely ones. She created walls with her husband before he died and she also created walls with some friends. She regrets very much how she handled her marriage in creating those walls and she does not want to see me make the same mistake. This is why she came. She does not want me going down the same path as she.

She is here to help me. Being twice divorced myself, she wants me to see the pattern that I am creating. That here is what I do and this is how it ends. Look at what you are doing.

She has watched me over the years, she knows me, and has every intention of staying with me until I make transition into her world.

"She's very fond of you," Sharon has told me. "She looks after you, she'll take care of you."

Agnes is a very positive presence and she enjoys living in this house with me. And after being on the other side, she has strong words of wisdom to offer. She also makes noise in the kitchen.

GREG: Ma-Ryah, I want to ask you. How does Agnes do it? I had moved four times in the last fourteen years and Agnes has found me each time. How does she find me? How does she know where I am? Does she look for my body? Does she follow my energy? There are so many people in the world. How does she pick me out?

MA-RYAH: ...*Sound! She follows the sound of you.*

GREG: The sound of me? I didn't know I had sound. I always thought of myself as a quiet person.

MA-RYAH: *Every human being, every spirit, you vibrate with several sounds, several tones and that is your fingerprint of spirit.*

No matter where you are, when you send out thought, when you are just existing, you create harmony or discordance among humans, are your tones compatible?

THE SPIRIT OF JONATHAN

1841-1851

Jonathan is a ten year old boy. He lived from 1841 to 1851, and during that time frame he was given the name of Jonathan Wilcox. He is dressed in short pants just below the knee, a coursed shirt and bare feet.

As a human being, Jonathan was very much a boy of ten years old. He was very active, loved the outdoors, enjoyed getting dirty, and loved animals.

He was born in England but his family moved to America when he was a baby. They settled in New Jersey in the area of New Brunswick.

He died in 1851 from the combination of the measles and serious wounds on his legs which he inflicted on himself in an accident with an ax. He was helping to cut down a tree when he severed his thighs on both legs. The combination of the measles and the wounds to his legs caused him to make transition at his young age.

Jonathan still carries those wounds around with him that he inflicted in that time period. He does not have to be seen like that but he chooses to do so.

Jonathan came to live in my house back in 2001 because of Agnes. He found her, and just like old friends who hadn't seen each other in a while, they met up and he decided to stay. He and Agnes apparently had been spiritual friends for a long time.

In my house, Agnes is like a grandmother to him. They communicate and have conversations and she will cook for him and he will perceive that he is eating.

"Jonathan can make a lot of talk," Agnes once mentioned.

When strange occurrences began to happen around our house, my son and I had much difficulty putting the pieces of the puzzle together. For me it became an obsession. I needed to find out what was going on, who was behind all of this. The lights would flicker, things would appear, then disappear, things would move, the electric to the entire house would shut down, and there was a drawing on a bedroom wall.

Later, we came to find out that it was Jonathan. All of the strange occurrences happening in the house was all the work of Jonathan. This ten year old boy was desperately trying to get our attention. He wanted to be acknowledged and have his presence known. It became obvious that things in this house were not right, but as a human being, when these types of things are happening, it's much easier to turn your head, ignore them and dismiss them as nothing.

Jonathan visits every room of the house. He is upstairs, downstairs, living room, dining room, my bedroom, my son's bedroom, kitchen and the porch. I *was* reassured though that he stays out of the bathroom. Agnes makes sure of that.

Jonathan's real job in the spirit world is to be a transition guide for children who are about to cross over. When a child dies, they are greeted by many other children on the other side welcoming them... full of innocence, love, encouragement and peace. And they invite the child to play. Jonathan is one of these spiritual child greeters.

Jonathan was very much loved by his family during his short life from 1841 to 1851, and currently he is very happy and content living here in this house with my son and I. He enjoys the love that he receives from Agnes and he is delighted that my son and I continually acknowledge his presence.

THE SPIRIT OF SARAH

1920's

The spirit of Sarah is a four year old girl. She lived and died in the period of the early 1920's, and during that time period she was given the name Sarah Taylor.

Sarah is wearing a 1920's child style of dress, she has big bows in her hair and shoes that have buckles.

As a human she loved baby dolls, music, flowers and coloring with crayons. She was shy and somewhat withdrawn by those who didn't know her, and here in my house she spends most of her time upstairs.

Sarah was very much loved and enjoyed by her family and now in spirit, she has Agnes and she has Jonathan. She very much likes living here with my son and I and she says that the house is very quiet when I'm not home.

She died of Scarlet Fever which went to her heart and then spread fluid to her lungs. She was four years old.

It was suggested to me that whenever I have music playing to invite Sarah to come downstairs and join in with the music...to feel free to dance, and that it's alright to do it. Feel free to let your presence be known and that I am really alright with it.

With her, it is easier for her to allow energy of herself to be seen when she is in the moment of joy with music.

Because of her shyness and her withdrawnness, I have to constantly remind her that I do very much enjoy her being here and that she is very welcome to let herself be known.

Sarah is in spirit but is very much attune to human beings and the happenings on earth. She spends a lot of her time listening, observing and processing. It's almost as if she has one foot in spirit and one foot on earth as a human.

I didn't realize at the completion of the last book that Sarah was a shy, withdrawn child. I also didn't realize that she doesn't come down the stairs unless she is invited. I suddenly felt like I needed to give her some extra attention. So, at times when the radio was on in the kitchen, I would invite her down and tell her that it's okay to join in with the music. "You can dance to the music Sarah. It's alright, I don't mind. Come on down."

Realistically though, I would often forget. In addition to that, I'm busy. I have a career to tend to, a son to look after, and maybe I just thought the whole thing was silly.

I did little things that I thought were meaningful but yet were quick and easy for me. I placed three rag dolls on the stool in the corner of my bedroom for her. During the spring and summer months I keep fresh flowers on the upstairs landing table. I'd speak to her every now and then to let her know that I acknowledge her and do enjoy her being here, and every once in a while I would sit on the edge of my bed and play the guitar for her thinking that she will hear it. Sometimes I felt very foolish doing these things but I did them anyway.

FLICKERING LIGHTS

Things have quieted down when it comes to Jonathan. Things are much more subdued now. It's not like it was a year ago when the lights in the dining room would go crazy having a complete mind of their own.

I remember being in the dining room. I would see the light out, but as soon as I turned around, the light would go on again. I would turn it off and moments later it would be on. It was like an argument. I wanted the light off and the lamp wanted it on. And then it would go crazy going off and on very fast. It wouldn't stop, and it happened night after night. I later found out that it was Jonathan doing it. I was always curious as to how he did that.

GREG: Ma-Ryah, how does he do it? Is he standing there next to the lamp turning it off and on while watching me? Does he use his hand to do it with? Is he waiting for me to not look when he does it?

MA-RYAH: *No, no. When he is making light flicker he is like child running, running around saying look at me, look at me, look at me.*

GREG: He would always do this around the same time...

MA-RYAH: *Yes, You are there. You are waiting for it. You are looking forward to it.*

GREG: So he's running around the dining room...

MA-RYAH: *Yes, he's running, running. Jonathan is gifted in communication. He does not require too much encouragement. He is able to let his presence be known.*

10

But a year has passed now and he really doesn't do much of that anymore. He doesn't play too much with the lights or the electricity to the house. Things don't move like they used to or appear and disappear. He doesn't feel he needs to get our attention like that. He knows that he has it.

However, that doesn't mean that occasionally he doesn't let me know that he is around. Jonathan is very gifted in communication and if he has a desire to let me know he is with me, he will find a way to do it.

I was told that Jonathan travels with me much more out of my house now, and on one particular night, he let his presence be known.

SMILEY FACES

On the back of my bathroom door is the picture of a smiley face. Actually, it's on the spine of the door where the front meets the back, the part that's hung up by hinges. On that part of the door about three quarters of the way down is this picture. It's almost as if the paint has chipped off or has been scratched into what I know to be a smiley face. There are two eyes and a round curvature for a mouth.

Joey discovered it. It's not very big but it's there. It is the only chipped paint or thing scratched out on the entire door and it happens to be in the shape of a smiley face.

During the summer months I work nights as a bartender in a local restaurant. A couple of those nights I wait on the waiters and waitresses only. They come to me to get drinks for their tables. During those nights, I have eight servers coming to me from one side of the bar and four others coming to me from the other side of the bar. My job is to be available for both.

One night in July 2006, one of the waitresses had approached me after having read my book and persistently asked me if anything else had happened. She was particularly interested in Jonathan and if there were any more drawings from him. My immediate response was, "No, there hasn't been."

I then thought a minute and said, "But there is something that my son discovered." I explained to her that there was a peculiar picture of a smiley face that was scratched out or chipped into the shape of a smiley face on the spine of the bathroom door. "I don't know if it's him." I told her. "It's just there," I said. "For me to say that it is Jonathan would be ridiculous. I can't confirm that. It's just something that we noticed and it's very much there. It would be a stretch for me to say, 'Oh yes, that chipped paint is him drawing a picture of a smiley face for us to see.' That's crazy!"

Anyway, we talked about the book a little and about Jonathan and how he is a bit of a character, and then she left to tend to a table that had just been sat in her station.

On the other side of the bar was a drink order that was waiting for me. The order consisted of two vodka and tonics, a screwdriver and a pint of draft beer. I made the drinks, put them up on the bar along with the ticket for the server and then went on doing whatever else I was doing.

Two minutes later, the waitress Gail came up to me laughing with a look of amazement in her eyes.

"Oh my gosh!" she said. "Did you see that draft beer that you poured?"

"No. What do you mean?" I asked.

"The draft beer that you just gave me. My table couldn't believe it. They even took a picture of it," she said.

"They took a picture of it? Why?" I asked.

"Because the foam at the top of the beer was in the shape of a smiley face."

JOE

As my son Joey got older I thought it would be best to stop talking about the three spirits that live with us. He was now in sixth grade with his own set of problems to deal with. I tried not to bring up the ghost stuff unless he brought it up and wanted to talk about it.

I know that he enjoyed reading his name in the newspaper and occasionally he would ask me about Jonathan and Sarah. I would tell him what I knew at the time and would then drop the subject.

I know that there are things that have scared him. I know that he has heard footsteps up and down the steps, the metal of the dresser handles have rattled during his sleep, there was heavy breathing in his right ear while he was alone upstairs, and other little things that he has commented on.

"Things always happen when I'm alone," explained Joe.

And I'll tell him some things that have happened to me around here briefly, but what I've found is that with everything else on his mind such as school, back and forth to mom's house, wanting to play with his friends, he often is not as interested to hear of the ghostly happenings at Dad's house as he once was.

THE SESSIONS

When Sharon comes to my house, she sits in the yellow winged back chair in the living room and I sit on the couch aside from her.

Agnes, Jonathan and Sarah are always present. They listen to the conversations and sometimes they are the only ones listening. Other times however, there are many other beings present. They are very much drawn to the energy that is happening at the time and they come to join in.

Some come to listen and some come to be heard. What ever the case, it is mostly people from different time frames, the 1600's, 1700's 1800's, men, women, children and animals, each dressed in their own time periods. According to Ma-Ryah, these types of meetings attract beings from all over.

Ma-Ryah doesn't always tell me what's going on, probably for my own well being. Not all that she sees is good and it's probably better if I don't know, but when she is looking around the room and laughing out loud, I often hope that she will tell me what it is that she is laughing about.

GREG: Ma-Ryah, I'd like to ask, I've noticed that sometimes when I ask you questions about Agnes, Jonathan or Sarah you start to smile and even laugh a bit. Are they doing funny things?

MA-RYAH: *Sometimes they are doing funny things. Most of the time it is because they are filled with joy because we acknowledge their presence. Right now, Jonathan is dancing...in your dining room.*

GREG: Are there any other spirits in the room with us now besides Agnes, Jonathan and Sarah?

MA-RYAH: *Yes, this is a very full space. Whenever there is this type of communication, there are beings that gather from everywhere. There is nothing that would be considered fear based here.*

GREG: Can you see them all?

MA-RYAH: *Yes, we do...*

GREG: Are they in a physical form or...

MA-RYAH: *We see some in the physical. We see some as energy who do not have or never had a form and as we leave they will also leave. And the only ones that will stay will be the ones that came with you or any that you would invite to stay.*

GREG: When you are speaking, I notice that you are looking all around the room and you may smile at one point, hold your hand up almost indicating, 'wait or hold it' at another point. You are nodding at different sections of the room, then another hand gesture to another area and so on...

MA-RYAH: *Yes, you will notice whenever we are communicating with you, I look all around you and nod, do hand gestures, heart gestures, because there is so many beings that are present and they all want the focus on them.*

GREG: Everyone wants a little attention.

MA-RYAH: *Yes. They are delighted to be seen and many have words for your world, but yet the human that is here is not the one the words are for.*

GREG: Has anyone come through to visit lately that I might know?

MA-RYAH: *Yes... Jonathan's mother will come to see Jonathan from time to time, and Agnes' husband will come to speak with Agnes and to see how she is doing. And your great grandfather comes to see you every once in a while. He comes to see what you are doing.*

GREG: Really? I have a picture of him hanging up in my dining room. He was a magician in Vaudeville.

MA-RYAH: *Yes, he comes...chiseled face, broad shoulders, performer...*

GREG: So he's interested in what I'm doing?

MA-RYAH: *Yes, very much so.*

GREG: If Jonathan's mother comes to see him, why doesn't she want to stay with him? Why wouldn't she want to stay with her son?

MA-RYAH: *Because she does not choose so much to be around the earth. So when she chooses to connect with him they spend time and then she returns to the realm which she exists.*

GREG: How long does Agnes' husband stay with Agnes?

MA-RYAH: *Maybe a few days your time, then he moves on.*

GREG: Where is Agnes right now?

MA-RYAH: *Agnes is in the dining room there.*

GREG: Can you tell me who else is here?

MA-RYAH: *You have a desire to know who else here?*

GREG: Yes, I would very much like to know who is in my house with us now.

MA-RYAH: *Over by your cabinet there in the corner with the glass, there is also a chair that has been created. A big back chair that a man sits in.*

He has vest, watch, such very dignified, very refined man. We are seeing him in his time frame where he is known as Samuel Jackson.

17

Next to him is child...little female seen about two years of age. She stands and she has one hand on his leg...and her name is Emily. She does not know beyond Emily. She has dark of hair and very cherub face, very round face.

You also have two woman what would be seen as sitting at chairs at your table there. They are from the 1700 time frame. One in the chair here is woman is named Ophelia Filany is her name. Next to her is a mistress of Geraldine Defray.

Standing there next to table is also canine that is like um...you use now as four legged officer...German Shepherd. He travels with Ophelia there.

There is also sitting here by wall is infant. And sitting there the infant is masculine child recently left physical world. His name...already he does not remember for he is infant. His name... Charles Thomas James. He is of Africa decent and he is birthed into this world with tumor. They are not able to sustain his life. He leaves and he is not yet six months of age. So he is here. So if you hear like baby cry, it will be him and to know that Agnes will already physically taking care of him.

GREG: Will he be staying here?

MA-RYAH: *Not for long.*

GREG: Not for long, is that a couple of weeks my time, couple of months?

MA-RYAH: *Perhaps about a month, two months your time. It is only a matter of letting go of the costuming and there is not a lot of identification so it will not take long to let go of earth.*

GREG: Now the others that are here...the man with the vest, the women sitting at the table, the cherub faced girl...they are here just because you are here?

MA-RYAH: *The man with the vest, yes because we are here and the child next to him. The rest they are...they are not going to like so much what we are saying because it does not go along with what they are perceiving. They do not see so much this time frame. And so they have created especially the women at the table...they have created what is an eating establishment and they do not see so much that this is home in this time frame. They see it more like a restaurant that one is able to go into.*

The infant there, is knowing that Agnes is able to help him and so his spiritual guide brings him to Agnes.

Canine is drawn because of the woman. It was her canine when she was physical. So that just like when you drop away the human life, there is certain ones who meet you and they will present what they know is able to be received.

And this woman she is not so happy as human being and she creates in a way to push people away. She stands behind a great shadow of aloofness. And all that she connected with in a loving way was the animal kingdom.

GREG: Now when you leave, will those women be staying or going?

MA-RYAH: *As long as you are alright with it, they will stay for a while.*

GREG: I'm alright with it. How about Agnes? Is she okay with it?

MA-RYAH: *Oh Agnes does not mind at all.*

GREG: Is there anyone here that is fear based?

MA-RYAH: *No there isn't, and Agnes will take care of that unless you consciously or subconsciously invite one to stay. If that occurs Agnes will not interfere.*

GREG: Okay.

MA-RYAH: *You have someone sitting next to you now who is being silly.* (Ma-Ryah smiling, laughing)

GREG: Who is sitting next to me?

MA-RYAH: *She is woman. She is here just because she is drawn to the energy right now. She most likely will not be staying.*
She in your world would be seen as someone who makes money in pleasuring men. She is very sultry woman.

GREG: What is she doing?

MA-RYAH: *She is...* (Ma-Ryah giggling).

GREG: When I'm talking to you...do the spirits listen to me? Do they comment on what I say?

MA-RYAH: *Yes, very much listening and they do comment. Some of them make good comments.*

GREG: Have there been times when some of them tell me that I'm ridiculous for asking some of the things that I ask?

MA-RYAH: *Yes, some do. The women at the table aren't paying too much attention to it and are only occasionally looking at you. But the sultry woman. She is making laughter at you.*

GREG: What is she doing?

MA-RYAH: *She is...mocking you and mimicking every gesture and facial expression you make. She is imitating you.*

GREG: ...Alright.

MA-RYAH: *And now you have man that just came in who has very much body mass...white* hat...*white gloves, he cooks. So he and Agnes may spend a little time together. You may hear a little more of sound in the kitchen in the next couple of days and then he moves on.*

GREG: So they come and go.

MA-RYAH: *Yes, it is...another world. If you only had awareness of their sight, you would see, there is not a lot of uncovered space.*

GREG: Did they make full transition?

MA-RYAH: *No, They are still here and very much still attached to this plane, this earth. There are many reasons for their staying, each not for the same reason. They are considered earthbound as you say.*

GREG: Have they chosen to stay?

MA-RYAH: *They chose at this time not to move on.*

DANNI

MA-RYAH: *We are seeing a woman now...standing in doorway of your kitchen. She is young woman. We will tell you what we are seeing. She is 14-15 years old...she just told us she is 15. She is... African slave from 1700's period of time.*

She has ropes tied around her wrists and the ropes are cut. She was tied down when she was killed. She did not die peacefully. She just showed us how she was put to death.

If you were to see her height, she is about 5 foot 4, very, very thin. Not a lot of body mass to her in that time frame. So she would been seen about 90 lbs.

She has her hair is very long and she creates the braids and she brings the weave hair back and it is covered with cloth tied...here around the head here.

Her clothing is very poor...very plain dressed...light grey colored from neck to here and she wears clothing protector...apron, so it covers the body all the way to the floor. No shoes on her feet...is always without shoes.

There is scaring and blood on her face.

Her name in that time frame is...Danielle, but is too painful to be called that anymore. She wishes not to be called that but instead to be known as Danni.

GREG: Did she just appear there in my kitchen? Why did she come?

MA-RYAH: *She had been standing there listening, watching. She came because of Agnes. Her spiritual guide directed her to Agnes. Agnes can help her.*

Danni was standing in the doorway leading into the kitchen next to the picture on the wall. Agnes was in the dining room between the window and chair, Jonathan was now in the living room sitting on the floor, and Sarah was halfway down the steps peaking from behind the railing.

MA-RYAH: *Danni is asking you can she stay in your house until she re-enters for another incarnation around eight months your time.*

GREG: Yes, she can stay.

MA-RYAH: *She would like that very much. Danni sees how you are with the children. She never met nice white man. She also asks if is okay to sing. She never was allowed to sing as a slave.*

GREG: Yes, she can sing if she wants to. Will I hear it?

MA-RYAH: *You will hear it when you least expect it. You will be preoccupied with other things...but you will hear beautiful singing or instrument playing. You will not so much be paying attention to it.*

There is a lot that she doesn't know so Agnes is going to help her prepare and assist her with that and to help her. There are times when you may feel her energy on the left side of your body. It will be the feeling of a chill on the left side of your body. It will be Danni not getting out of the way of you fast enough.

Your house is beginning to look like halfway house for spirits to reenter.

GREG: Yeah and it looks like Agnes is working the front desk.

MA-RYAH: *Yes, very much like that.*

It was that evening, all the windows and doors were shut and the heat was turned up to a warm 72 degrees. While standing in the dining room, a cool gentle breeze swept across the left side of my face.

SHE'S BEHIND YOU

Something very unexpected happened to me in the summer of 2006.

I was in the kitchen. I had just sat down on the stool near the old red brick chimney near the entrance way to the dining room. It was early evening–6:00 p.m.

I was sitting there enjoying the moment for whatever it was and was losing myself in the warmth of the sunlight coming in through the kitchen window.

Suddenly, out of nowhere, I got the feeling that someone was behind me. It was the kind of feeling that someone is watching you and that they are behind you. It came upon me very fast and it was very strong.

I turned to look and as soon as I did I let out a gasp as I'm sure my face turned white. In the air floating above the floor was a long blue dress.

"Agnes?" I called out.

My heart was pounding while my eyes widened. And then that quick, she was gone. The shock of it kept me from seeing more. I had lost the vision of her.

This experience may have only lasted for two seconds but she was there and I saw her. I'll never forget the vision of that dress.

Aside from that incident, I don't always know when Agnes is around. I know that the kitchen clock stops and starts on its own all of the time. I keep changing the battery but it doesn't help. I can't attribute that to Agnes or Danni yet, I just know that the clock never has the right time on it.

But Agnes is quiet for the most part, and it's my understanding that it's intentional. It is not her intention to scare me or startle me.

It has to be difficult for her because she very much wants me to know that she is around but yet she doesn't want to do it with the element of surprise to scare me. She's not going to stage any kind of jaw dropping event to get my attention just to let me know that she's around.

MA-RYAH: *Were you aware two nights ago, your energy was low, she made much noise in the kitchen...around the area of the sink. She was trying to get your attention.*

GREG: No!...did I react to the noise?

MA-RYAH: *Only slightly, you turned to look, but only a little bit..."*

It's these types of things—the small stuff. I'm getting to know it, what to look for, how to perceive it.

Seeing Agnes though was fantastic. How many people get the opportunity to actually see a live spirit? The best way for me to describe it is that her dress is blue. It comes down below her knees but yet a foot off of the floor. It very much looked like clothing from the early 1900's.

There is white braided trim around the base of the dress as well as on the ends of the long sleeves and around the collar. I remember thinking that the trim around the base, sleeves and collar was made of quality. It looked a little dirty but was certainly of detail and it was just there. I'll never forget it.

I had to go to Ma-Ryah. I didn't tell her what I had seen or the experience that I had, I just wanted to know what Agnes is wearing.

MA-RYAH: *Yes...she dresses in like a 1920's period of clothing for length and such. She wears more subdued colors than she does bright colors. And the dress that she wears most of the time is a very subdued what would be like mostly blue and some grey mixed together. And...she has white cuff around here and around the bottom base of dress here and up around collar here.*

She wears her hair up and she wears... mmm...I don't know what it's called, silhouette of face on broach, that she has a ribbon around her. She does not truly manifest shoes and such.

GREG: Oh my gosh! She was right behind me by the old brick chimney in the kitchen. She was right off my right shoulder. You just described to me what I had seen. That's what I saw her as wearing. The white braided trim, I'll never forget it. It was around the base of the dress, the sleeves and collar.

I didn't see any ribbon or broach with a face on it, but I know what I saw.

MA-RYAH: *Well good then, you can celebrate that you are indeed beginning to see her.*

GREG: ...But I wasn't even trying to do that. It just happened.

MA-RYAH: *Yes. Once you have set out your intention that you have done, that you desire to see her and you have sat to perceive her, then that energy stays unless you were to say to her that I do not desire to see you. Unless you say that, she takes it still as green light to communicate.*

THE VESSEL

By now, you may be asking yourself, who is Ma-Ryah? And for this, I have to start from the beginning.

Lou Ann is my next door neighbor. Lou Ann has four sisters. One of Lou Ann's sisters is named Sharon. Sharon was born with psychic abilities, and she has been a medium, a channeler and a sound healer for over twenty years. This is what she does for a living.

Sharon and I met in the backyards of my and her sister's house. I didn't know at that time that Sharon has had the ability to speak with ghosts and spirits since she was nine years old. She was living in New York at the time but came to see her sister for a visit in Somers Point, New Jersey, who happens to live right next door to me.

I knew that she had a special gift. I just didn't know the extent of it.

The best way to describe her talent would be to compare her to the boy who sees dead people in the movie the *Sixth Sense*, or to Jennifer Love Hewitt who plays Melinda Gordon on the Tv show, *"Ghost Whisperer."* Sharon has this ability in real life.

It was a summer day when I just happened to meet her. In looking back, the timing of it was very strange because it was right around the time when I was having strange things occurring in my house. It was almost like we were supposed to meet, like it was supposed to happen.

She read me briefly in my backyard and some weeks later she came through my house. Later, I hired her to come over and do the channeling for me which was to tell me exactly who is in my house and what is going on.

It is then that Sharon brings in her spiritual guide named Ma-Ryah. While entering into an altered state of consciousness, Sharon is able to willingly relinquish the use of her mind to Ma-Ryah's thoughts, and Ma-Ryah is then able to activate and move Sharon's body and speak. I am then able to talk to Ma-Ryah one on one and ask anything that I want to ask.

Human beings are only of the 3rd dimension and Ma-Ryah is of the 7th dimension. Agnes is of the 5th dimension.

Ma-Ryah has never lived as a human being here on earth and even though she sees, hears and understands this world with remarkable detail, she has no interest in living here.

Because Sharon has the ability to be the "in-between" or translator between the human world and the spirit world she is therefore referred to by spirit as, "The Vessel," basically because she is able to drive the information from one world to the other.

The entire process of meeting with Sharon and then speaking with Ma-Ryah one to one is very easy and not at all scary. Actually she is a lot of fun to talk to.

Ma-Ryah is extremely polite, knowledgeable, witty, sensitive, caressing, loving, genuine and reassuring. When you talk to her it is almost as if she is holding you in a warm blanket and telling you that everything is going to be alright. She is caressing with her wisdom and reassuring you that all of the pain, negativity and suffering you are experiencing on this earth during this lifetime, is for the betterment of your soul, it is about learning. And even though you may be filled with hatred, anger, guilt, or shame, what you really are is an ultimate being of love and light who is full of goodness and kindness.

She has told me things about myself that no one could ever know. She has told me things about family members and friends, and that there is a purpose for our lives and for our existence. There are people benefitting from you being here. You never know who you are influencing or when.

You can ask Ma-Ryah anything and she will give an answer that no one living on this planet could give. Every word tells something, explains something about our world and the existence of human beings and for the reason and purpose for our lives.

Before meeting with her I am prepared with about twenty open ended questions as well as many other short answer questions. Ma-Ryah sometimes can get through my questions very quickly. She really doesn't need to think about them. And if I asked her a question now, and then in two months ask the very question again, her answer would be the same with very few words changed.

However, she is not loose with information. She will only give answers to something that you have a desire to know, ready to hear, and willing to accept. She is not going to tell you anything that would have a negative impact on who you are today in this moment of time. She is here to guide and to help, not to hurt, distort or derail your destined path.

She is very aware of what humans are allowed to know and what they are not allowed to know, and what is permissible by spirit. She knows how much she is allowed to tell.

This is one thing that I weigh very carefully and have to decide on before asking a question. Am I ready to hear the answer? Can I handle it? Ma-Ryah reads my energy to know if I am ready or not.

I remember having a lump in my throat when Ma-Ryah told me how my death will occur in this life. She told me what to look out for, the place where it will happen, who will be around me at the time, and the ultimate cause of my transition. She also told me that my transition will be very fast and very strong. She gave me this information because I really wanted to know. It was permissible by spirit for her to tell me and she felt that I could handle it.

So, with that in mind, is there anything that you would like to ask Ma-Ryah?

APPLE PIES

GREG: So...how did Agnes feel about me seeing her?

MA-RYAH: *She is very excited.*

GREG: She is?

MA-RYAH: *Yes, very much so. Shortly after you had that awareness of her, do you have remembrance of the scent of apple pie?*

GREG: Apple pie? No, I don't.

MA-RYAH: *She will do more for you. Whenever she is celebrating herself as Agnes and there was a happy day for her, she would create apple pies, so that those who have known her...that is her signature, her gift that others knew that if Agnes was happy, they had happy stomachs. She will work on helping you to smell her pies.*

She uses a bit more nutmeg...she's giving you her secret ingredient. She adds a bit of the fresh rosemary. The rosemary works as an awakening for the smells.

So a little more nutmeg, a little more cinnamon and a little bit more rosemary. People would say, 'Wow!' What a wonderful pie you have made.

GREG: Ma-Ryah, for a while there when I would sit down at the computer, sometimes to write, I would feel a tickling in my hair...almost like there was a bug in my hair only I knew it wasn't a bug. Is that Agnes?

MA-RYAH: *It is us (spirit). We are just letting you know that we are there and around, and that we are seeing you.*

GREG: Is it you Ma-Ryah that's touching me?

MA-RYAH: *Yes, it is Ma-Ryah touching you on the top of head briefly.*

WINDOWS, WALLS AND MIRRORS

Back in 2004 when things started appearing and disappearing around the house and I knew something was going on, I had gone to see a tarot card reader in central New Jersey. She not only told me that I had an older woman and two children living with me, but that one of the children likes to draw. She suggested that I start paying more attention to mirrors, windows, walls and dirt outside the house.

About one year after that happened, my son and I had awakened to a drawing on a bedroom wall. It was a line that measured six and one half feet across the wall. It was dark and it looked like pencil, only it wouldn't erase. Joey had crawled into bed with me during the night and discovered it on the wall the next morning. He woke me up with great excitement to see.

When Sharon was over I took her up to the bedroom to look at it. She told me that the boy Jonathan had drawn it and then Ma-Ryah later confirmed that it was a picture of a city.

In early June of 2006 I painted over Jonathan's drawing. The room needed to be painted and that meant that the line had to be painted too. I did give it some thought, and after some consideration of leaving the line as a memento, I decided not to. I painted over it.

I used three coats of paint to paint over that line. I painted the room using only one coat of paint but used three coats over Jonathan's drawing. If I had decided to paint over it, then let it be gone.

With new paint and a shuffling of furniture, the room looked good. And Jonathan's drawing of a city was nothing more than a fond memory.

It was late July of 2006. I was shocked when I awoke to find that the drawing of Jonathan's city, the one that I had painted over with three coats of paint, was back on the wall. It had bled right through the three coats of paint and seemed to get darker as the days went by.

His drawing was now just as visible as it was when it first occurred a year before. It looked the same, just as it always did.

I later learned that Jonathan's drawings are permanent. Once they are there, they are there for good. And when he is present, he can manipulate his drawing to appear darker or lighter, but there is no getting rid of them.

It's really quite simple. When he wants me to know that he is around, he will make his drawing appear and when he is not around, the drawing will fade away into the wall.

As for me on the human side of things, this is why I would see the drawing as coming and going. I thought it was the sun coming in through the window or a glare or something that would provide some sort of scientific explanation. But no, it was simply Jonathan telling me that he was here and he wanted me to know it.

Spirit ended up telling Jonathan not to do anymore drawings because it is a permanent marking on the wall which is not beneficial to me. Maybe I showed concern at one point, I don't know, but I really didn't mind.

It was then that Ma-Ryah told me that only if I give permission to Jonathan to allow him to do that, will he be allowed again by spirit. That I must okay it and approve it for him to be able to do it.

I told Ma-Ryah to tell him to go ahead, he can draw whatever he wants. I don't care. It will make for good conversation. I'm not planning to sell this house, so if the room is filled with Jonathan Wilcox's drawings than so be it.

"Go ahead Jonathan, draw whatever you like. I'm really fine with it," I called out to him.

While looking towards the top of the stairs, Ma-Ryah smiled. She then whispered that Jonathan was smiling also.

Next time, he's planning to draw not just a city or buildings on the wall, he will draw other things as well.

CHANGING SEASONS

During the fall of 2006, I can't recall too many things happening around the house. There are very much periods of quiet and it seemed like during that fall was one of them. That was however until Thanksgiving.

The past few years I have hosted Thanksgiving at my house for my family. It is the one time of year that the entire family gets together to celebrate a holiday. There is always plenty of food, adults talking, children playing, and pictures taken.

It was around this time when the presence of Jonathan and Sarah began to surface again and in many of the pictures were large white orbs, particularly around the staircase area.

In one of the pictures was a white orb which had the image of a little girl in it. It was ghostly. Who was the image of in that picture? Is it Sarah? In the orb the little girl was wearing a hat and a white ruffled shirt looking from the era of the early 1900's.

It was later learned that it was not an image of Sarah but instead an image of Sarah's doll. Sarah was showing everybody in the room her doll at the time. And at that moment the camera just happen to snap, and it was caught on film.

A CHRISTMAS ORNAMENT

That following December as it was getting close to Christmas, I learned that both Jonathan and Sarah had a desire to have an ornament for the Christmas tree. Something designated for them only, so they would feel part of the family. Something that they could call their own and that I would always remember them by. I considered this to be extremely worthy. I got my coat and went out to shop at the malls.

I wanted to try and find something unique, maybe a bit odd, but definitely special. So that whenever I would look at it, I would immediately think of them and only them.

After going in and out of stores and coming out empty handed, I stumbled upon a small booth in the center of the mall. The woman was selling hollow ceramic white molds that she had made into ornaments. She told me that when they are near the lights of the Christmas tree that they will light up and give off a subtle inviting glow.

I looked around at her display and found one that I thought to be appropriate. It was a white ceramic mold of two children in angel wings.

"This is the one." I said. "I'll take this one."

"Would you like something written on it?" The woman asked.

"Yes, would you please write Jonathan and Sarah on it."

"The older woman picked up her calligraphy pen of gold ink and carefully wrote the names Jonathan and Sarah on the back.

When I got home that afternoon, I wanted Jonathan and Sarah to see what it was that I was going to hang on the tree in their memory. So I called them both down from up top of the stairs and presented the ornament to them. I showed them the front of it and then turned it around and showed them their names written on the back in gold ink. I then turned to the side and hung it on the tree.

The truth is, I felt kind of ridiculous doing this. I mean I was talking to the bottom of an empty staircase. I couldn't see them or hear them. I didn't even know if they were in the house at the time. And if they were, had they even listened to me and come down like I had invited them to. But anyway I felt like I needed to do it. I showed the empty staircase the ornament, I said a few other little things out loud and then hung it on the tree.

At my next session with Ma-Ryah, months later, I asked Ma-Ryah if Jonathan and Sarah were in the house at the time and if they were aware that I got an ornament in their memory.

GREG: Ma-Ryah, I invited them to come down the stairs so I could talk to them and show them what I had bought. I'm not even sure what I said and I felt a little silly doing it. But I did it. Did they even hear me?

MA-RYAH: *Oh yes...very much so. They were very much listening. Jonathan was at the bottom of the step here...and Sarah was half way down.*

GREG: Do they desire anything else?

MA-RYAH: *No, they are both very content.*

CANDY DISH ON THE VICTROLA

New Year's Eve came two weeks later. The next day would be the year 2007. I didn't have any plans, wasn't going to go out. I was just sitting in the living room watching the Tv when out of nowhere a small holiday Reese's peanut butter cup fell out of the candy dish and landed on the floor in the dining room. It seemed to just fall out of nowhere. The candy dish wasn't even full. There was nothing that would have created it to fall. I was the only one home. It just fell out of the candy dish. It was very strange how this happened.

I walked over to it, picked it up and put it back into the candy dish that sits on the old antique Victrola in the dining room.

It was then that I noticed that right behind the candy dish, I had placed a picture of my grandmother who had died twenty-seven years ago.

It then occurred to me that it was last New Year's Eve, this exact same day exactly one year ago, while standing in the kitchen, I was drinking out of my dead grandmother's champagne glasses that she had given me. I yelled out, "Happy New Year Grandmom and thanks for the glasses." It was just then that one of the bulbs in the track lighting system blew out making a loud pop.

This year, a small candy fell to the floor completely out of nowhere. It was very peculiar. It was then that I walked over to it and saw my grandmother's picture facing the candy dish.

OTHER STORIES...

Kitchen Candles

I was sitting on the stool in my kitchen. I had the old brick chimney to the right of me and the refrigerator to the left. It was around 9:00 at night. Sitting on the counter top were three candles. I arranged them in the shape of a triangle, having two at the base and the third one above them. They were sitting on the glass cutting board next to the sink, and they were burning beautifully.

I called the local pizzeria and ordered some food. I was told by a worker that there was no delivery that night. All food ordered had to be picked up.

The pizza shop is less than two blocks away. Picking it up was never a big deal. But it's hard for me to blow these candles out. It's almost like I'm magnetized to them. The way in which they were burning, it was like they had a charismatic glow to them, they were so peaceful and inviting. And I knew that I would only be gone a few minutes while I went to go pick up my order. I foolishly decided to risk it.

Just as I walked out the backdoor, I turned my head once more to look, then closed the door and darted through my backyard on my way. I moved quickly as I knew the candles were burning in my house.

I got to the pizzeria, paid for the food, and then ran back to the house even faster than I had started.

I walked into the backdoor and luckily found nothing on fire. The candles were still burning as they were and everything was safe. They were exactly the way that I had left them burning evenly and beautifully.

"Whew!" I said as I sat back down on the stool. "I'll never do that again. That was a stupid thing to do," I said to myself.

It was then that I experienced one of the most frightening things that have ever happened to me here. I had only been back in the house a few minutes just sitting on the stool when out of nowhere, at exactly the same moment all three candles went out. It happened at precisely the same moment. There had been no movement of air. Both the window and door were closed shut, and the house was still and quiet.

The room went dark except for a little lamp that sits on the kitchen counter top.

My hands trembled and my heart pounded as I gasped for air. And for the first time through all of my experiences in this house, this one had me shaking.

In addition to the oddness of this occurrence, even stranger was the fact that right after the candles snuffed out on their own, there wasn't even the slightest glow to the wick and not even the faintest sight or smell of smoke. It was almost as if a giant vacuum had come down and just sucked everything up.

The only thing that I could assume was that Agnes wasn't very happy with me leaving the house with the candles lit.

GREG: Ma-Ryah, does Agnes try different things to get my attention?

MA-RYAH: *Yes, but very little gets through. You are not an easy person to get through.*

Voice in My Sleep

It was around 4:30 in the morning. I was just about asleep when I heard it. It was very loud and very clear.

Someone called out my name. It was a woman's voice, friendly but strong.

It woke me up in a jolt to the point where I rose my head up from the pillow to quickly scan the room. Nothing was there–at least I didn't see anything.

My heart pounded as I tried to catch my breath. It was difficult for me to get back to sleep after that.

MA-RYAH: *Sometimes when you are in the twilight sleep. You're not yet asleep but yet you are no longer awake, that is easy time for spirit to talk, for you to hear them. The challenge for you will be to be able to stay in that twilight and not jerk out of it.*

Mouse Trap Mystery

During that winter of 2007, I had found mice droppings in the kitchen near the trash area. I also found them underneath the sink.

I suspected they were living behind the refrigerator and washer and dryer which sit together along the kitchen wall.

I bought a D-Con unit of mouse food and put it behind the refrigerator. I placed it as far behind the refrigerator that my arm could reach. I then pushed the small box off with my finger tips.

Three days later I had looked at it and noticed that the food was gone. I was glad that the mice had eaten it and was confident that this would solve my problem in getting rid of them.

I bent down to pick up the empty mouse food trap but I couldn't reach it. When I had pushed it off with my finger tips behind the refrigerator, I didn't think about trying to get it back again. It was too far back, far beyond my reach. I was now going to need a pole or a stick to help me get it out.

My patience for this project however had already run out. This was a three second job which had now gone into its second minute of trying to reach this thing and throw it away in the trash. "Forget it." I said out loud to myself. "I'll get it another day." I left it there and went on to do something else.

The next morning I walked into the kitchen only to find the empty mouse food trap that was completely out of my reach out from behind the refrigerator and about one foot away from the wall.

Tugging on My Shirt

I vividly remember standing in the entrance way of the kitchen just about to walk into the dining room and having the feeling of tugging on the back of my shirt. It then felt like the back of my shirt was being pushed in. It was a very strange feeling. There was no one there, but it was happening and I am certain that I felt it.

On another occasion, I was sitting at the computer doing some work as I watched my pant leg make an indentation right above the knee. It was a very warm comfortable feeling. I didn't think much of it. But I watched my pant leg close in on its own. I also felt it on the skin of my leg as it pressed in.

GREG: Ma-Ryah, something new has started. I have felt at times tugging on my shirt and then it felt as if the back of my shirt was being pressed in very easily and gently. Three times I have sat at my computer to watch indentations happen on my shirt and my pants. I start to feel it and then I look down to see it happening.

I never experienced this before. I don't know what's going on but it has my attention. I can't jump to conclusions but I am very curious to know what this is...if anything.

MA-RYAH: *Yes, it's Jonathan.*

GREG: It's Jonathan? He's touching me?

MA-RYAH: *Yes,* (big smile) *he's wanting your attention. He's sitting on your lap and giving you hugs. Jonathan is very loving of you.*

AGNES' MOTHER

Something very sobering happened the following spring. How quickly things can change. This news started me thinking about how lucky I was to have had this experience.

I very much remember it being a cool sunny day and I was on my way to Sharon's house. I pulled in her driveway. She was outside petting her dog Angel. We talked briefly and then went in. She had some candles lit on the coffee table and her tape recorder was set up. The tuning forks were unraveled. She was ready to go. So was I. I was very excited. Getting read is extremely exciting to me, and I had very much been looking forward to this one. Sharon brought Ma-Ryah through and we talked for a while. I had a few questions about random things that had nothing to do with ghosts or spirits. I think we were talking about the effects that coffee has on the liver. And then we talked about tea. We then got to my list of questions about my house guests.

GREG: Ma-Ryah, has Agnes been trying to communicate with me in the kitchen?

There was a long pause in Ma-Ryah's response. In fact there was no response. Ma-Ryah did not speak. Her eyes were fixated on the light fixture which hangs overtop of Sharon's dining room table. Ma-Ryah was nodding to the overhead light fixture as if she understands what the light fixture is saying. Ma-Ryah was looking very serious in her demeanor and I was growing more and more uncomfortable. What was going on?

I suddenly felt anxious. My head was going back and forth. I kept watching Ma-Ryah to the left and watching her talk to the light fixture toward the right. She wasn't saying much but her eyes were glued and she was doing a lot of nodding. I had no idea what was about to come.

Ma-Ryah then began to speak. The tone of her voice however was different. It was now a voice of concern. The laughter and excitement had disappeared for now as she started to explain to me what was going on.

MA-RYAH: *The woman of Agnes is in quite a quandary right now. She has been getting visits from her mother. She is thinking about leaving you.*

GREG: Agnes is leaving?

MA-RYAH: *The one who is seen in the time frame as her mother is speaking to her to go farther, to let go, that you are different than you were when Agnes first came to you.*

She chooses to stay because of you and at this point she has chosen to stay with you until you make transition.

...And a lot of what was your truth, no longer is. You still carry the shadow. You still carry the seed of it and yet you are more conscious of it. So that you do not require her to be there to assist you.

Agnes' mother said that I have learned the lessons that I needed to learn and that it is time for Agnes to move on. Her mother has been visiting, inviting Agnes to be born again with her as twin sisters.

Agnes' mother has been contacting Agnes for about the last month or so. Her mother has already picked out the parents.

GREG: So Agnes is getting visits from her mother and her mother is trying to persuade her to move on from me, to let go, that I have learned what needs to be learned.

MA-RYAH: *Yes.*

GREG: So Agnes' mother has been in my house.

MA-RYAH: *Yes.*

GREG: Does Agnes want to do this, be born again with her mother as twin sisters?

MA-RYAH: *Yes, she does. As sad as her other life was experienced as, it's joyful the one that she will step into. She and her mother choose parents this time who are very aware and who are very much conscious of who they are in the world and supporting the souls of them.*

And as a coming of twins, she and the mother have much time to adjust and create in the womb as their energy becomes part of the fetuses. So they have both a joyful life to experience.

But yet, part of her hesitation was her knowing how sad, was her last one. So...we will assist her. Agnes finds herself in a self induced quandary because she has made this commitment even though you have not heard from her herself, the words of commitment. To her, her word is her word.

You may notice purple lights around your house over the next few days. We are going to communicate with her. If she chooses to completely let go and re-enter life, she will let you know that this occurs.

GREG: So how will she let me know?

MA-RYAH: *You will have awareness of someone by your bed that is not Jonathan or Sarah. She will leave the kitchen area of your home to let you know. You may experience it in a dream state, or you may experience it in the twilight and you will know when she chooses to leave, if that is indeed her choice.*

GREG: Is she listening to our conversation now?

MA-RYAH: *Yes, she is by the light fixture there.*

GREG: So you were talking to Agnes. Agnes told you that her mother was visiting.

MA-RYAH: *Yes, it is Agnes.*

I understand if she has to go. I'll miss her but it sounds like it's best for her and probably the right thing to do. Is she listening to me say this?

MA-RYAH: *Yes.*

GREG: I say things to Agnes often in the kitchen. I talk to her and tell her things. Does she listen to me?

MA-RYAH: *Very much so!*

GREG: Are there times when she wants to respond to what I am saying but she can't?

MA-RYAH: *Yes, but she does speak. You just don't hear her. She does speak. It is very much just a matter of fine tuning and we understand that it is frustrating for the human being. But it is a matter of being open and you are open. It is a matter of being comfortable that you might be startled and indeed you are able to be startled when you hear. And it is the willingness and the joy with it and you have both. So you have all of the basis covered.*

In the years of linear that she has been with you, you are like son to her. She is very much loving of you. And so it is the same tearing of mother from son. It's difficult for her and yet she

47

also is looking forward to re-entering and being twin with her mother.

So... Agnes is...is very torn. You'd think being in spirit it would be easy for her to choose. Not so.

It was upsetting for me to hear that Agnes was leaving because as odd as it sounds I always felt some comfort in knowing that she was around. She wanted to be here; she wanted to help. I am grateful for that. But at the same time I understand now that she must go.

This all started because she wanted to talk to me about the destructive pattern that I am on with loving others.

If I hadn't met Sharon on that day I may have never gotten to hear her opinions, her observations, and her wisdom.

But Sharon and I met, I became aware of Agnes and I heard Agnes' words for me. Her words of wisdom would only benefit me for the rest of my life, and I listened very carefully.

I understand now that she needs to move on and if she chooses to go than I will accept that. It is not something that I want to accept, but will have to.

It sounds like she has a wonderful opportunity waiting for her if she wants it.

I drove home from Sharon's house that day thinking about the conversation, and when I got home I took out some paper and a pen and wrote down some of my thoughts. It actually ended up to be a long thank you letter of three pages to Agnes. I thanked her for coming, for all that she had done and for the lessons I had learned. I told her how much fun it was and that I found great joy in her presence. I wished her well on her next endeavor as she moves on.

I tried not to think about it much as the days passed by. But all the same, I was very much saddened by it. I didn't want her to leave. I wasn't ready for her to move on. Plus, I think it was difficult for me to accept the fact that she was leaving voluntarily. I'm already a twice divorced man and now the woman in my life from the spirit world is leaving me. I was feeling down and my energy was low. I thought about talking to someone about it, but who will listen. Who could really understand.

Trying to explain to someone that the reason you're upset is because your ghost is leaving you, is not an easy conversation to have.

SARAH'S DRIFTING

Upon my next visit with Sharon, I had a desire to know more about Sarah. I had been thinking a lot about her and I wanted to know how she was and what she was doing?

GREG: Ma-Ryah, how is Sarah? Can you tell me about Sarah. I've been giving her a lot more attention. I'm wondering if she knows it. Does she hear the guitar I play for her and is she listening when I say things to her?

MA-RYAH: *Yes she hears you some of the time. (Long Pause) ...but we're not seeing Sarah's energy very strongly. She is not always there as before. She's coming and going. She is drifting.*

GREG: She's drifting? What does that mean?

MA-RYAH: *Sarah is considering entering a cycle again. This is an indication that Sarah is preparing to re-enter.*

GREG: What...re-enter? You mean she's going to be born again somewhere too? She's leaving too?

MA-RYAH: *Yes, she is ready for another incarnation. Sarah had been preparing for this, for re-entering into another life here on earth. She was in spirit but was very much attentive to the happenings to the world on earth. She was very much observing and listening and processing. She is ready.*

GREG: That's terrible...I mean I'm losing all of my ghosts. I know that comes off as sounding selfish, but...I mean...I thought...is Jonathan upset about Sarah and Agnes leaving?

MA-RYAH: *It is not what he chooses but he knows and understands.*

GREG: Is Jonathan leaving too?

MA-RYAH: *No. Jonathan is very content with you.*

GREG: Is Jonathan here? Is he with us now?

MA-RYAH: *Yes, he is sitting right next to you. If you want to see him, his head, you see where the cushion next to you has that curvature. He is like child sitting next to you and his head comes to this side (pointing to side). He is sitting there with you.*

I turned my head to the right to see and I also reached out my arm to feel. The truth is I saw nothing and felt nothing. In fact as soon as I reached out my arm, I quickly pulled it back again when it occurred to me that I may be passing it right through Jonathan's body.

MA-RYAH: *Jonathan would like to know...I'm speaking for Jonathan now...Jonathan would like to know, are...if there are any plans of you and your son having a canine?*

GREG: A canine...you mean having a dog? Well...no! We have fish. Actually, my son and I have talked about getting a dog. We've discussed it and he has told me that he really wants one but the problem is that there is no one home to watch it during the day. I work during the day and Joey is in school. There is no one to take care of it. It would be left all alone. There would be no one to let it outside or give it any attention. For that reason I thought that it would be best if we didn't get one.

MA-RYAH: *Jonathan just gave sad face.*

GREG: So...you mean...Jonathan wants us to get a dog?!

51

MA-RYAH: *Oh yes, very much so. Because when you were saying it would be all alone and you couldn't let it outside, Jonathan was saying, 'No it won't. I'll be here...I'll be here.' But he's not able to open doors and such.*

Also, you are able to...he is pleading...and you do not have to respond to it. Jonathan has 'Boppy' which he can see if he wants to."

GREG: Boppy was Jonathan's dog?

MA-RYAH: *Yes... your son also would very much like you to have a dog.*

GREG: I know, I know, he's wanted one for about a year.

MA-RYAH: *...I'm speaking for Jonathan now, you are able to create a fence in your yard.*

For a few seconds I just needed to enjoy the exchange of words and absorb the conversation. It's so funny to think that our spirit kid wants us to get a dog. I sat in silence for a moment. I thought about it, looked to the right of me, and then lowered my head with a smile.

LAST CHANCE

I was a bit distraught now that both Sarah and Agnes were leaving. And Sarah...I was really just getting to know her. To me, she was the one that I knew the least. And I was really hoping to see her one day, to have that opportunity to see her in her buckled shoes, her 1920's child style of dress and the bows in her hair. Ma-Ryah once commented that she is a beautiful child.

MA-RYAH: *...But there is a chance that you might be able to see her.*

GREG: There is? How?

MA-RYAH: *The Vessel, here, has training in hypnosis. You might be able to see her.*

I need to go under hypnosis? Hypnosis? It was explained to me that if I go under hypnosis and into a deeper state of conscience, that it is a good opportunity for spirit to connect with me, I would see more, hear more, and feel more. I would have a chance of not only seeing Sarah, but possibly Jonathan and Agnes too. It is not absolutely certain that I would, but there is a chance and I admit, I was tempted.

But what else is going to happen? What are the side effects? I've heard things about people who were hypnotized. That they have been taken advantage of while being under. That there are mind games that the hypnotist will play and what if I never come back?

At the same time, I had a very strong desire to see them and I figured that this was going to be my last chance.

"You always come back," explained Sharon. At the very worse you will just fall asleep. This could be very beneficial for you."

Sharon knew that I really wanted to see them, and she offered to drive to my house so I could be in the comforts of my own home during the session.

I agreed. Sharon and I made the arrangements and on a cloudy Sunday afternoon she knocked on my front door.

I wouldn't let just anyone hypnotize me. But I know Sharon and I trust Sharon. She is a good person and she knows more about me than anyone I know. I am comfortable with her. I was very nervous in doing this, but if I didn't, I was afraid I would have regret.

HYPNOSIS

Sharon walked through my front door relaxed and smiling which helped me to relax. We talked a while, and then it was time.

I couldn't help thinking of what would be revealed. Would I have flashbacks of being in the war? Would I begin speaking in a different language and...would I see my spirits.

I laid out on the couch in a comfortable position as Sharon suggested, and she then started talking to me in a calm soothing voice to get my body relaxed. She told me that I may hear the traffic outside but it won't bother me. I will hear other distractions but won't be distracted. I will be aware of it, but it won't have any effect on my thoughts and my deeper state of consciousness.

As I lay on the couch, Sharon was next to me kneeling on the floor by my side. She then started reciting some relaxation techniques to put my body fully at ease. And with the combination of her calm soothing voice and the words that she spoke, it worked. I became totally relaxed. She then told me as she counts to seven, with each number that she speaks, that I will fall into a deeper layer of consciousness until I eventually find myself in a meadow.

I could hear her and I was listening to her, and I was very relaxed, but after thirty minutes I still didn't feel like anything was happening. I was still at the same level of consciousness that I had always been. Nothing was happening. I wasn't going any deeper.

Sharon knew how to do this and she did her best in trying to get me to go but I was fighting it. I didn't want to go any deeper. I was afraid. I could not let myself have that vulnerability.

Hypnosis was a disaster. It didn't work. She tried but I did not want to lose the control. I wanted to be aware of where I was and what I was doing. I was stubborn, I blocked it and I kept it from happening.

When it was all over, I felt kind of bad. Sharon gave up her afternoon and went out of her way to help me with this and I blew it.

"It's alright," said Sharon. "Letting go is the most difficult thing for most people in hypnosis. We are all so used to keeping it together and are afraid of what will happen if we let go of that control."

"Yes, I didn't want to lose that control. I didn't want to feel vulnerable," I said. "I feel horrible though Sharon. You came all the way up here to help me and I resisted."

"Well it was your first time," said Sharon. "I'll tell you the one person who was really happy about you doing this," said Sharon excitedly.

"Who?" I asked

"Agnes!" she said.

"Agnes? Really?

"She was right here (pointing next to couch.) She was right here watching. She came out of the kitchen area to see. She was very excited," explained Sharon.

"Well I'm glad that Agnes liked it. I'm still embarrassed about it," I told her.

"Ah, don't feel bad. There were times actually that you were just about to go. I could see it in your face and then you popped out of it. You just would not let yourself do it," said Sharon.

"The same holds true for people afraid to come to channeling to meet Ma-Ryah. They are expecting an experience based on the human beings in their lives and seldom have an experience with a being that is unconditional love. They are afraid of what she will see when she looks at them, and what fear that she will expose. But that's not Ma-Ryah's intention. She doesn't expose any of that."

"Ah...pretty soon you'll be a pro at hypnosis," said Sharon.

"If you say so..." I said reluctantly.

My attempt at hypnosis was a failure. Sarah is leaving and I am image less. Perhaps it is supposed to be that way. I don't know. I just know that I would have loved to have seen that little girl.

FILLING THE VOID

I started to think that maybe getting a dog isn't such a bad idea after all. Jonathan is still very happy here and it looks like he is going to stay. That means it is going to be me, Joey and Jonathan living here. "You know what?" I told myself. "It's time to get a dog."

Joey and Jonathan both wanted one and maybe it would fill a void for me.

Plus it would be a very good experience for my son to have one. It would teach him about responsibility and the work involved in keeping a pet.

I started looking in the newspapers under the classified adds to see what was available. I also visited some of the local shelters to see what they had "in stock" and if it was the right dog for us.

I thought that finding a dog would be easy. It wasn't. I learned that some puppies cost from $500.00 on up. There were some even listed for over $1,000.00. For a dog? I didn't need that. I just wanted something that would be good with children, and not disturb the neighbors by barking a lot. Do I really need to spend a lot of money to have this?

I didn't have a lot of knowledge about dogs and had to do some homework. After researching and talking to people about it I started leaning towards a retriever. My sister has one and it is a nice, quiet, gentle dog. This was what I was looking for.

Months of searching had gone by but I kept coming up empty. I didn't have a lot of money to spend and the shelters had nothing that I considered to be a good match.

In the meantime, I continued to call the shelters, rescues and watched the ads in the papers. I filled out adoption applications to get early approvals just in case something came up and I talked to as many people as I could to find out who was having puppies in the neighborhood. What kind and how much? All of this resulted in nothing. We were dog less. It was frustrating and tiresome but at least I could tell the boys that I tried.

CAPE HATTERAS 5 MILES

Cape Hatteras – 5 miles. This is the sign that hangs on the shed in my backyard. It's just a decorative little sign but I've been noticing something lately. Something has been happening with it.

On clear sunny days when there is no wind, the sign very often will lean or tilt towards the left. I will straighten it, and then shortly afterwards, find it again leaning to the left.

I could easily blame it on the rain or wind or whatever weather was happening at the time but the sign will lean to the left when the weather has been peaceful and when there hasn't been the slightest bit of wind or rain. It can be a day of bright sun and still air and the sign still leans to the left when I'm out in the backyard.

I couldn't help to think if it was Jonathan doing it. Is he out in the yard with me?

Just the other night, the weather was terrible. We had a horrible rain storm, gusty winds, and downpours. I woke up the next morning to find the Cape Hatteras sign as straight as can be. It didn't move at all through the foul weather the entire night.

I became extremely focused on this sign. In the morning when I would leave for work, it would be the last thing I would look at before backing out of the driveway, and it would be the first thing I would look at when pulling into the driveway. I just couldn't make heads or tails of it.

I remember on a Saturday afternoon just standing there in front of the sign absolutely dumbfounded. It had tilted to the left right after I had just straightened it moments before. There was no wind, no clouds, not even the slightest breeze in the air. I couldn't believe it. "How is this happening?" I asked myself. I walked over to it and straightened it.

Then, for some reason, that was the last time. It all seemed to stop. The sign remained straight for weeks without moving.

It's been two months since the last time that it tilted and I had straightened it. It has now been straight through heavy rains, heavy winds and even on the calm sunny days. It still had gone unchanged.

INTUITION

Within a few days a strong urge had come to me to drive to the animal shelter. In fact I was driving down the highway when something just told me, "Go to the shelter." The shelter was a quarter mile up the road. I followed my instinct. I pulled up, went in, and talked to the lady behind the desk. She took me back to see the dogs that they had on the premises and it was then that I saw her. It was a beautiful black retriever mix who sat quietly in her kennel while the rest of the other dogs participated in a barking frenzy. This particular dog was scared to death. The woman was trying to lead me to another dog three kennels down, but I had to stop to read about this black dog sitting in the corner. The card posted on her kennel said, Black Retriever mix – female. Two and a half years old. Found running around the streets of the Villas.

The Villas is a small town in Southern New Jersey.

Then at the bottom of the card it said, "I am very afraid and I don't belong here."

She was so quiet, and so scared sitting in that corner that I knew instantly that I could give this dog a good home and that it was the right dog for us.

I took her out for a little walk to let her get familiar with me and again I felt strongly that this was the dog that we were supposed to have.

I told the lady at the shelter that I was very interested in adopting her. She then made up a card to post on her kennel. The card said, HOLD! for Gregory Young. Will pick up next Monday.

I was excited. I was also very relieved that my search was over. I had finally found a dog. I couldn't wait to tell

Joe. I knew he would be excited. And for me, it felt like a great burden had been lifted off of my shoulders.

I pulled into my driveway on that mild sunny afternoon, I quickly got out of the car and walked hurriedly toward the back door of my house. I wanted to grab the phone to call Joe. It was then that I happened to glance up at the shed to notice that the *Cape Hatteras 5 miles* sign was leaning towards the left like it had never leaned before.

SHADOW

One week later Joey and I went down together to pick up our dog. She had been in the shelter for a little over a month and the employees there had given her the name of Shadow. Joey and I decided to keep the name. It seemed very appropriate for a scared dog all black in color.

I don't think our dog does anything out of the ordinary in our house. She's not a big barker or growler and she's very polite and gentle. You know the question comes up, can the dog sense anything around the house? And my feeling is that she does the same things that every other dog does. Her eyes will focus on something and her body will freeze up sometimes in the bedroom. But she doesn't do anything too out of the ordinary. Joey however, sees things differently.

"Dad, she's too still," Joe insisted. "There are times when I'm up there with her and she just stands still. You can't even hear her breath, and she doesn't blink. Her eyes don't move, but then her head starts to move like she's watching something when nothing is there," Joey explained.

I *can* say that she is very clingy and doesn't go anywhere in this house without someone with her. If I walk up the steps she is right by my side. If I go into the kitchen, she goes into the kitchen. She follows me everywhere and does not want to be left alone- ever! However, that doesn't mean that it is because of the spirits living in the house. She may not even sense them. Some dogs are very "clingy" anyway.

However, there is one thing very peculiar that she will do. At times she will stand right at the base of the staircase with her tail between her legs. Then her head will lower. She just stands there very still and very quiet. It's almost as if she becomes a stuffed dog. She doesn't move. She looks scared but yet very much at peace at the same time, and it lasts for about five minutes each time that it happens. It's odd.

GREG: So Ma-Ryah, I finally found a dog to bring home. I found her at the shelter. Joey loves her. I'm wondering what Jonathan thinks of her.

MA-RYAH: *Jonathan is very happy. When you are not home, he is very much around canine. And when canine appears in deep sleep, Jonathan is very much loving her, cradling her, stroking her. He is very happy.*

GREG: There is something a bit peculiar that the dog does. Maybe you can give me some insight on this. There is something that happens at the bottom of the staircase that has caught my attention. There are times when she will stand at the bottom of the steps and just stand there for a long time looking somewhat scared but yet very much at peace at the same time. She just stands there and doesn't move.

MA-RYAH: *Yes, Jonathan is there with her. He's stroking her. That's Jonathan.*

THE PRESENCE OF DANNI

Danni had said from the beginning of her arrival that she would remain quiet, for she was not allowed to make much noise as a slave. She would also keep a clean house and not disturb any of my belongings or create the movement of objects. However, there have been a few times when she has let her presence be known, some are innocent and subtle, and some a bit more disturbing.

One of the more subtle things that she will do is manipulate the large Sauvignon Blanc sign hanging in the kitchen. I've come home a few times to find it crooked hanging on the wall. This sign is large and had always remained straight until the arrival of Danni.

MA-RYAH: *Yes, it is Danni simply to letting you know that she is around.*

The kitchen clock hanging on the wall – again I don't know if it is Agnes or Danni but the clock always stops and then restarts hours or days later. It never has the right time. Ma-Ryah says that it is just the energy in the room from Agnes, Danni and who ever else might be visiting at the time. It's the energy that is causing the clock to stop and that the clock itself is fine.

In late April, I came home to hear the singing of a woman's voice in my kitchen. It stopped though shortly after my entering the door.

MA-RYAH: *She tickles the end of your nose at times.*

But the most startling occurrence happened in late March 2007 involving some dishes. I had left dirty dishes in the sink from the night before. They had been sitting there for a little over twenty-four hours and I just didn't feel like washing them. I was even too lazy to put them in the dishwasher. Instead I just chose to stand in the kitchen, lean against the counter top and look at them.

Shadow was lying on the floor near me. She was halfway on the oriental style kitchen rug and halfway on the hardwood floor. She's not a huge dog but for some reason she finds a way to take up a lot of space.

I was becoming hungry. I opened up the refrigerator to find a left over foil wrapped cheese steak from the other night. I figured it was still good to eat. I decided to turn on the oven and heat it up.

Lying in the sink at that time were dinner plates, silverware, a frying pan with a glass lid a few bowls. The sink was half full.

At this time, the kitchen was quiet. I was very much caught up in my thoughts and shadow was dozing off lying on the floor.

I remember leaning against the counter top looking down at the floor when out of nowhere, the dishes in the sink crashed. It was almost as if someone had literally picked up all of the dishes and dropped them again, smashing them down into the sink. It was extremely loud and just seemed to happen while I was standing there.

I jumped I was so shaken by it. Shadow jumped as well. She rose quickly to her feet frightened by the sound and ran out of the kitchen.

My heart pounded from the loud shock and I immediately began searching for a reason as to how this could have happened. After all, the dishes had been sitting in that sink undisturbed for a good twenty-four hours.

The sound of them crashing was so strong that I was very surprised that nothing broke. I thought that I would find pieces of glass everywhere. Miraculously though, nothing had broken.

I immediately put the blame on Agnes. I know that she tries very much to get my attention in different ways and maybe she thought that she will finally get it if she makes a lot of noise while I am standing right next to her in the kitchen.

It wasn't until one month later though that I found out what had really happened. During that time of my cooking my cheese steak, when Shadow was peacefully lying on the floor and I was leaning against the counter top was the same time that Agnes and Danni were also in the kitchen next to us having a conversation.

During the conversation Danni was telling Agnes that because she is a slave and still living her life as a slave that she is very used to being quiet and not to bring attention to herself. Agnes however, was telling her that she can hold that template of the appearance of who she is but she no longer needs to hold the limitations and restrictions that she created. And that she can do more now because she is free. And that she no longer has to live the life of Danielle anymore.

Then Danni says, well then if that is true than I can do this..., Danni then picked up the dishes and crashed them in the sink.

Agnes then reminded her that it is not necessary to scare or startle.

WHO'S COOKING?

Another disturbing occurrence happened during a time when Danni helped cook on the stove. I had rice cooking on the front burner placed on low, and a can of gravy was poured into a pot on a rear burner. The gravy was not turned on because I never cook the gravy until the rice is completely finished and taken off of the stove. I then leave the pot of rice covered and place it on the glass cutting board.

I know how to cook my rice. It's the same routine each time. One and a third cups of water to half a cup of rice. That is the ratio. I cook it on low for about twenty-five minutes or until all of the water evaporates. Then I remove the covered pot and place it on the glass cutting board next to the sink. Then I heat up the gravy and pour it over the rice.

On this particular evening, I had the gravy in the pot ready to go but had not turned it on for the rice wasn't finished.

The rice was on low and I was back and forth from the kitchen to the living room watching, *The Antique Road Show* on Tv. I would go check on the rice every three minutes or so just to make sure everything was alright and then would go back to the living room and wait to hear the history of another item.

I was much disturbed however when I went back into the kitchen for my third trip of checking on it to find that the rice had been turned on high. I then turned my attention to the rear burner to find that the gravy had also been turned on high and at this point was boiling over.

I figured that it was Danni who manipulated the stove. Agnes has never done anything like that before. I immediately knew that this had to be addressed.

"Danni?" I spoke out. "Thank you for trying to help me as I'm sure you know how to cook. But please don't cook in the kitchen without me being there. I'm very afraid that the house might catch on fire."

Since then, nothing like this has happened. However I keep an eye on the stove a little bit more than I used to. I have a feeling that Agnes may have had a talk with Danni also.

A more innocent occurrence happened while I was standing in the kitchen. I was hearing a thumping sound coming from one of the upstairs bedrooms. I figured it was coming from my son's room because that is the one right over top of the kitchen where I was standing. It was like something was banging or thumping. I heard it twice in the same minute. It was almost as if something heavy had dropped to the floor. At that point I was too nervous to even go up there. This was one of those times when I found it easier to ignore it than to pay attention to it and deal with it.

Again, I thought that this was Danni doing something. I was wrong however, and it was Danni who came forward to claim her innocence. Danni explained that the thumping sound coming from upstairs was Jonathan playing with a ball in Joey's bedroom, and that it wasn't her at all.

A REVIEW

GREG: Ma-Ryah, am I right in saying that Danni is an earthbound spirit?

MA-RYAH: *Yes, what you would see as earthbound. We see it as not making full transition. She still very much is still holding on to the life that she just lived in the 1700's. Agnes will help her.*

GREG: Okay...so let's say that I go into the light and I make full transition. Do I then get to choose where I want to go? What happens then?

MA-RYAH: *Ultimately, you are born back into spirit which is your true home, and you go through a review.*

GREG: A review. What is a review?

MA-RYAH: *It is a review of the life that you just lived as being in the flesh. What did you create? Did you create love or did you create fear? It is not about how many trophies you won or how many books you read, it is who did you effect and how did you effect them? Where you loving of others?*

GREG: How long does a review take?

MA-RYAH: *Sometimes what is seen in linear is able to take years. It all depends on the way the human created life. The more they created fearful of love, the more they have to review. When the soul reviews you are seeing your entire existence and you are seeing each moment that you created outside of love.*

...Say that you have a very challenging day at work and your mood becomes very dense, very negative. You leave your work, you stop at store. You are short in temper with the person in store. You get back in car and continue on and each person you meet you give them a piece of that negative self.

In the review, you are aware of what you received, what you felt. You see the interactions between you and the person in the store.

What is different at that point is then you are the person in the store and you see what you did as that person to the next being.

GREG: So in the review, if I were to yell at someone on my way home from work, during the review, I am now the other person. I am receiving all of the negativity of the person yelling which is me when I was in that situation on earth. I am learning what it felt like to be on the receiving end and how it affected that person for the rest of their day or week or whatever...

MA-RYAH: *Yes. Because now you can see that you may have upset that person and then that person who received your yelling now goes home to their family feeling despaired and then they may take that out on someone who is at home ...a child perhaps or spouse, who are undeserving of it...and the ripple effect goes on and on.*

We spoke the one time and said that the human that designed the first gun, when he has his review, he reviews the creation of the gun and we will speak of only Winchester at this point, so that when he has his review, here is what he sees as the benefit of creating the gun. It has many benefits. It also has many negatives, fearful aspects.

So he had very long review because then he saw what was the use of the gun, what was the bullet, at the person that received the bullet and then receiving the family of the first person killed with the bullet and it goes all out.

GREG: So during a review of my life or the life that I just lived I am the receiver of me. And I then get to see how negatively I affected other people. It is then that I will have understanding of how it affected them and how they felt being on the other side of that.

MA-RYAH: *Yes. You think when you are done, the human part, that you are done the learning and the growing and it only just begins because then you return to spirit, to who you really are, which is only love and light. And to be able to see how did you apply who you are and how did you create who you are not.*

GREG: So is that then the real reason that we are here?

MA-RYAH: *The only reason as human beings you are here...there are always a myriad of sub reasons that each one chooses to experience of life, the main and most important reason you are here is to manifest who you are as spirit into the flesh without distortion.*

And who you are of course is unconditional love and that is the journey of the human being you create and you enter with separation and the planting of fear in order to allow that separation to be experienced.

And then you will work through what is seen as linear time to transform these fears until you remember that you are only spirit and you are only an expression of All That Is.

And what happens when you come here to earth, you forget and you believe you are the sum total of the things that as humans you have shame, you have regret, you have belief that you must somehow make it up in order to for you to be received back in spirit.

When you do something and then have regret, instead of beating yourselves up, instead to see what do you now know and understand that you did not know before you did that.

GREG: Well then...when I die, will all of that knowledge and wisdom that I learned during this lifetime be lost and then I have to learn it all over again? It starts from the beginning again?

MA-RYAH: *No, no. You are able to take it all a bit farther and it keeps growing.*

The goal of becoming aware of and conscious of who you are as spiritual beings, not only human beings is for that when you enter what is seen as the next incarnation, you enter with remembrance. You are able to see that in children. And the difference would be that you would not forget as most humans do now.

You would have remembrance. You would have more deja vu moments, that you have done this before, and be able to take that moment to be conscious.

What was my choice before? What do I choose now? The ability to ultimately enter into a life without any forgetfulness, no unconsciousness. What you do in spirit in between the lives you are also able to apply to remembrance.

ANOTHER LIFE

(Three Months Later)

GREG: Hello Ma-Ryah it's good to speak with you again. How are you?

MA-RYAH: *We are fine. It always nice when humans ask us how we are. It is nice to say always fine.*

GREG: I wish I could say that all the time. Is Danni still here?

MA-RYAH: *Yes, she is in the doorway there.*

GREG: And you had said before that she is wearing ropes around her wrists and that she was tied down when she was killed?

MA-RYAH: *Yes, but she does not have the ropes on her now. Only her wrists now are scared with blood and such.*

GREG: Why did she take them off?

MA-RYAH: *Because she understands that she does not have to carry that. Agnes does a lot of work with her.*

GREG: Kind of like showing her around, and how to do things?

MA-RYAH: *Yes, Agnes is very helpful to her. Agnes is...very proud of her house.*

GREG: Where was Danni a slave?

MA-RYAH: *She was slave in what was Louisiana of your world. If you were to see New Orleans, it would be the first community to the Northeast of New Orleans and...is not very large community when she is there. The building that she creates life in, in that time frame, is still there.*

GREG: Does she enjoy being here in my house and staying with us?

MA-RYAH: *Yes she does. She is happy that she does not have to be afraid to be seen and to be heard and Agnes is very mothering, loving energy for her.*
Agnes is also receptive to all other Beings coming and speaking with her. So she is open to those who assist her to let go of the earth plane. She has not even know what is long linear years. She has not ever gone into what you as humans say to go into the light. And what would be the review of soul and then by choice back and forth. She has not done that and so Agnes is preparing her to be able to be knowledgeable that she is able to go into the realm of love and then to return to the earth plane as she chooses...not stuck.

GREG: What is going to happen to her now? Where is she going to go after her eight months time with me?

MA-RYAH: *She is going to be born into an Asian family. She will be born boy and study music.*

GREG: Does she enjoy music?

MA-RYAH: *She likes the harp...the violin, she likes the sound of that. She likes the beating of the drum...very much drums.*

GREG: Has she ever heard me playing the drums downstairs?

MA-RYAH: *Yes, she has.*

GREG: Is there anything that Danni desires at this time?

MA-RYAH: *If you are able to have music with the violin she would very much like that.*

GREG: Alright, I'll see what I can do. I'll get it to her.

JOHN

GREG: Ma-Ryah, you had said before that we all have spiritual guides.

MA-RYAH: *Yes, at least one. Some people also may have a day to day guide which also helps.*

GREG: Well then if spiritual guides are supposed to be good, then why do some people commit such violent acts against others?

MA-RYAH: *Because they are choosing not to listen to their guides. They are instead listening to fear based beings who are not of love. The guides are very much trying to get through and to be heard but the human refuses to listen.*

GREG: How does a child of say...three years old know that they want to be a doctor or a fighter pilot when they have had no previous exposure with either one of those professions?

MA-RYAH: *Some young children are very aware of what they are here for and what path to walk. Sometimes they do not complete it and most often it is the awareness of what they chose before entrance or what they are willing to experience this time.*

The children are afraid of what is their world right now. There is very much pain right now in your world and it becomes greater before it begins to tilt again. Your world is a very frightening place for many and the children are absorbing it even if they do not speak. They are afraid.

GREG: It is a scary place. Ma-Ryah, can I ask you a question about my spiritual guide?

MA-RYAH: *Yes.*

GREG: You had told me that his name is John and he was my brother in a past life.

MA-RYAH: *Yes.*

GREG: Do I ever make him laugh?

MA-RYAH: *He laughs very often with you. If he were here in the physical with you once again as he has walked with you in other lives, he would be saying words to you to get your attention, to say, what do you think you're doing?*

Sometimes he is like parent shaking his head when you are having the experience of missed opportunities in having what you desire.

For him, it is sometimes he hits his head on the brick wall when you are putting from the mind reasons not to even begin to have an experience.

GREG: Sometimes I will do that. I will talk myself out of doing something because I've already predicted the outcome before ever even experiencing it.

MA-RYAH: *Yes, and he is there shaking his head because there is wisdom to be applied to every experience.*

GREG: Lately I've been seeing waves of movement in different rooms throughout the house. I'm wondering...

MA-RYAH: *Yes, when you are seeing like waves of movement, like ripples in the water, that's Agnes! She is the easiest one for you to see. Jonathan would be more of a swirling motion.*

PAST LIVES

GREG: So if I've had past lives with John, it sounds like your telling me that reincarnation is real.

MA-RYAH: *Yes.*

GREG: Well can you tell me, have I lived on this earth before?

MA-RYAH: *You have walked many times on this earth.*

GREG: Can you tell me anything about who I was? When I lived? Who was I?

MA-RYAH: *Yes, we can give you some knowledge.*
We see you physical in what would be seen as 600 period of time. In that time you are creating an area of what is the northern area of China. You are extreme poverty in that time frame. You are judged by the clubbing of the foot as well as the great poverty.

So when you have meeting of female that you desire to be with, first you are not able to be with her because of difference in wealth.

You are one who tends the fields, you are one who tends to the oxen. You are one who works entire life with nothing more than expectations of bowl of rice occasionally. You do not have material things and you have very small shelter to live in.

You do wed in that time frame and yet it is one that is without love. It is one that is chosen for you of similar poverty and one who works very diligently by your side.

Together you bring ten children into life. Only five make it to adult and so there is a sadness from that time frame that you are not able to have what you want. You are not able to have of your choosing that when you do create beauty, that you do not retain what you do create and so from there comes the seed that when you do bring love to you it disappears. It falls apart.

GREG: I still carry that around with me today. So that part of me was created in the 600 period time frame, which is still evident in the life I am living now.

MA-RYAH: *Yes, the seed was planted during that time period and one of your jobs in this life time is to try and transform it, to overcome it.*

Also, the wisdom developed and the ability to go within the life lived in that time frame was much solitude–working the fields, communication with that of the Gods and the thoughts and the awareness of cycles of nature. So that you are very much in tune with the flow of the world. You are able to receive much information from the earth that many would not receive because they did not work closely with it as you.

GREG: I've often been called "earthy." People have referred to me as being an earthy kind of fellow.

MA-RYAH: *Yes, this was developed in that time frame. So just as the seeds of shadow are planted in different time frames and are able to be accessed, so are the gifts.*

GREG: Seeds of shadow? Is that our fears, our insecurities?

MA-RYAH: *Yes, those seeds were also planted and they are the ones that need to be transformed.*

GREG: Does it show up in every life time?

MA-RYAH: *It is always there, but in some time frames, not always so evident.*

So you're able to tap into the intuitive self that is developed in that time frame, for one whose station in life was not to be very high in achievement.

There was in the depth of being contentment, not for wife though, the two of you worked well together. Neither received love and neither expected love.

The death of the children, three boys, two girls and remaining is four girls and one boy. So the death of the children in that time frame is equally difficult for both.

GREG: Okay, so I'm going to say this back to you.

In the year 600 I was a Chinese peasant working the fields all day long-basically my entire life. It was during that time frame that I developed strong ties with the earth and nature.

The woman that I wanted to be with I couldn't have because I was poor and she was not. In addition to that I also had a handicap of a club foot and was harshly judged by that. Therefore, a woman was chosen for me to be my wife. She was also a peasant. We had ten children together and half of them died.

So...from that life time...the seed that was planted in me was not to let anything get too close to me because I will only lose it in the end. Whatever I create, whether it be love or beauty, it will somehow be destroyed. And that it's easier for me not to love anything because if I do love something it will go away and fall apart.

MA-RYAH: *Yes.*

GREG: ...And because that is so much left inside of me today, one of my jobs in this life time is to transform it. It is called a seed of shadow because it is a negative and just because it happened in that lifetime doesn't mean it will happen in every life time. And this is one of the reasons why Agnes came to me, to help me to be aware of this shadow and to help me work on transforming it.

MA-RYAH: *Yes.*

GREG: Do you see any other lives?

MA-RYAH: *We are now seeing you in the 1700's. That time frame has strong bearing on this time frame. In that time frame you are seen as what would be ...um... understood as indigenous people of this land. In that of tribal knowledge you would be seen as what is known as the Apache band of peoples. You are residing in the area which is more as seen by now as...Mexico. Then the United States later became as now is Texas area.*

In that time frame, you desired very much to be chief of that which was the hunters, and to provide nourishment for your people.

And when you are hunting in the hunting party, your aim is very accurate, but yet often you would not see the deer, you would not see the buffalo, you would not see the bear until others began to go after it to shoot arrows for it to entrap it.

You were too busy in the mind day dreaming of when you are the chief, of that what you would be bringing to your people.

The reason that this time frame is so beneficial for you to know about is because you get the almost apathy in moving forward because you are tied up in the mind. And instead of being tied up in the mind which you are in that time frame, you get tied up in what if you do not achieve it, and so you very subtly begin to sabotage it, so you do not achieve it unless that shadow is validated and strengthened.

The meaning of your name in that native language would be "Walking Bear." And you received this name because you spent many days walking to find bear and to kill to bring home to the people, and it was so much in the mind that you were creating that you did not realize that there was a bear stalking you. It wasn't until the other members of the hunting party came upon you looking out over an area of the land looking for the bear. And here was the bear, it was behind you and you did not know it. So out of the humor, you were given the name of, "Walking Bear."

GREG: It is all so true. I get so deep in my thoughts. I'm very often oblivious and unaware as to what's happening around me. Many times it is like there is an amusement park of thoughts going on in my mind. There is so much going on and so much for me to think about. I'm always preoccupied and get lost in my thoughts.

And it's just like when I was Walking Bear. I did not see the deer, the bear, the buffalo, when actually I just wasn't paying close enough attention. The similarities are uncanny. I very often don't pay attention to things that are right in front of me.

MA-RYAH: *Yes, you are one who drifts in deep thought when driving. There are times when you cannot remember 15 minutes of driving. It is your spiritual guide John that brings you back.*

GREG: Is there a seed of shadow that I need to transform from that time period as my life as Walking Bear.

MA-RYAH: *Only to be more aware of it and to be more conscious of it.*

GREG: Alright. Any more past lives?

MA-RYAH: *We see you once again in the physical in the 1700's time frame, in the area that is England. You are in what is known as Sussex, like*

84

a county. In that area you are female child. You are not so well in the mind. You are not what would be seen as retardation and yet you are walking a fine line between being able to be seen as not able to care for yourself and yet able to be self sufficient. It creates much difficulty for you in this time frame because you are nice of face, little large of body and you are of home that is abundant, owning of land, owning of money, not real rich and yet very comfortable.

You are schooled in that time frame the greatest you are able to be schooled. In this time frame it is not usual for female not to be wed. For you, you are not able to be wed because you are not seen as being able to be sufficient. The reason that this time frame has bearing on now is because the feeling of not being sufficient to sustain a relationship. This is the seed that is planted there and it was daily reinforced.

In that time frame you make transition in your 42nd year. So for 42 years, you have reinforced daily that you are not adequate enough, so that when that thought arises in this time frame, to tell yourself that you are not Jessica this time and to say that you are Gregory this time and this will help align yourself with the differences.

This past life hit me hard. I very much still carry around with me many of those feelings- feelings of inferiority. It is suppressed in me but very often it surfaces in my life today. Many times I will second guess myself in what I am doing. I begin to feel very inferior or not as good as everyone around me. I feel like everyone is smarter than me, better than me, happier than me. These thoughts usually result in a deep hole for which I dig for myself. It leads to depression and usually takes a good four or five days for me to climb out of the hole. During this time, I don't eat well, I don't want to get out of bed in the morning, I'm very quiet and very sad. It is a depression. I hate this part of me, but every once in a while it happens and it is so hard for me to come out of it. I feel like during those times, I am regressing back to being Jessica again and experiencing the life that I once lived as her, those thoughts, those feelings, those emotions.

I need to keep my life as Jessica out of my life, but when things start going wrong, or someone says something negative to me, or about me, I internalize it and I instantly regain that feeling of inferiority.

I still very much have that awareness. I spent 42 years hearing that I wasn't good enough to take care of myself. That no man would marry me because of my special needs, that I was never good enough to count as somebody or to feel good about who I was. This seed of shadow, I very much know about and will probably be the most difficult for me to transform.

Maybe that's why now during this life that I am living, I have a constant drive to succeed and to be self sufficient.

So the three seeds of shadow that I need to work on transforming during this lifetime are?

1. My life as the Chinese peasant – To transform the shadow that if I create love, it won't necessarily be destroyed. So to stop building walls and pushing people away and instead begin to build bridges.

2. My life as Walking Bear – That I need to be more aware of what's going on around me, and to not be so busy in the mind. I am actually missing a lot of opportunities, new experiences, which could be very beneficial to me.

3. My life as Jessica – Don't keep myself down. Get rid of the feeling that I am inferior. I am not Jessica anymore.

MA-RYAH: *Those are the three strongest seeds of shadow that you create within this time frame. Your journey in this time is to transform at least one of them. If you transform all of them to a degree, that is wonderful. You are transforming the seeds of shadow.*

GREG: Are there lives that I have had that you are not allowed to tell me about?

MA-RYAH: *Yes, we are only permitted to speak of ones that you will benefit from.*

Spirit will not allow Ma-Ryah to tell me anything that will negatively affect my life today and disrupt the course that I am on. She will only share with me the lives that will help me continue on my destined path of ultimate love and light.

GREG: Can you tell me, was I in the civil war?

MA-RYAH: *Yes, we are able to give you some knowledge so you can see who you are in that time frame.*

You are African Being and you are woman. You are slave. The energy of the name that you have is that of Mason...Sadie Mason. So in the records for slavery in that time you will find records of Sadie Mason.

You are very young woman and you are on the border of South Carolina and Georgia in that section there, the large cities there.

In the second year of the war, in that moment of time you are given your freedom by the one who has owned you.

It was very difficult for you to be gifted freedom especially in time of war. You were young woman now on her own.

You seek to join with others and you are brought into more North but not full North because you are very afraid as what is seen in the Yankees and you settle in the area of West Virginia around what is now seen as the Norfolk area.

You study, you research the underground railway and you will find reference to Sadie Mason and you will see she lives to elder and you will see she is very instrumental in freedom passage of many other slaves.

GREG: How did I die?

MA-RYAH: *You die of old age. Your body just shuts down in your sleep.*

GREG: Ma-Ryah, this has nothing to do with Sadie Mason but I have a fear. I have always had a terrible fear of ladders, heights, I can't go on a roof of any kind. I was never one to climb trees or enjoy amusement rides. What happened? Can you give me some awareness of why I have this? Were seeds of shadow planted in different lives to make me have fear of these things?

MA-RYAH: *Yes, because you do not have it from this time frame.*

In the period of what would be seen as 1832, you are Caucasian male and living in the United States. You are traveling west. You have horse, wagon and such...and you make journey with wife, three sons and four daughters, and wife is growing another child. You are part of a small gathering of people together, not what would be seen as great wagon trains but a small gathering of people.

You are choosing to go to the area that is Utah now and you make through many of the areas that many Caucasian people did not make it in life for the indigenous people fighting.

And as you are coming down the mountains in Utah, your wheel on your wagon, it breaks. You fall and you are in death and wife and most of

88

children are also in death. You have two sons that are not with wagon, and they are walking ahead. They do not die. The rest of you die.

In your moment of death, when you are looking and knowing that very second when the wheel breaks is very narrow and it gets the wagon off just enough that you have that moment in life when everything stops and you see how far down it is.

It is not so much fear for yourself as it is your mourning and your sadness to deep knowing that your children in the wagon will die, your wife and your new baby and the growing will die. And your fear, for what's going to happen to the two that are walking ahead.

They ultimately are alright and they are absorbed by others you are going with, and they make it to your destination, and they become part of life in that area.

In your moments of knowing that fear of your family was so great. So you associate height with death and loss.

In my life today, I cannot go up on roofs, up on ladders or anywhere up high where I don't feel safe. I constantly check the tire pressure in the wheels of my car, make sure the locks on my doors of my house work properly, I always make sure I have gas in the car in case of an emergency. Always testing smoke detectors making sure that they work. It's all about safety and preventing an accident. I am compulsive in these areas, probably because I didn't check the wagon wheel when I knew that I should have, and my family died as a result of it.

GREG: Ma-Ryah, I have another question about something that has been bothering me.

MA-RYAH: *Yes.*

GREG: In my sleep I'm always reading newspaper articles. I can actually see the headlines of the column and then the words to the articles and I read them, but when I wake up I can't remember anything that they said or what they were about. But I'm reading them all of the time.

And also, I don't have a lot of tolerance for detail. When someone is telling me a story I want them to give me the facts and to get to the point. I want every word to tell me something. I don't like that about myself, but it's just who I am.

Are these two things connected in anyway? What is going on here? Is there anything you can tell me?

MA-RYAH: *Yes, you are male being in the 1934 period of time. You are Charles Kingston in the area of Indianapolis. You are very rough in that time frame. You are short with people. You are very much attuned to facts. You are journalist—news!*

A BUNDLE OF GRAPES

One of the most interesting things that I have learned from Ma-Ryah is what she teaches about the relationships between family members.

MA-RYAH: *Yes, you come as a soul grouping like a bundle of grapes and you just keep changing your position in it. For us the kaleidoscope is like the soul groupings. The pieces of it are exactly the same and do not ever change, and yet depending on how you turn it so that the mirrors create a reflection is how you take the souls at a slightly altered reflection you get a completely different experience.*

We are very much amazed in your kaleidoscope because we hear from humans all the time, what is the purpose of coming and coming and coming and doing it over and over, and in the way to explain it in the kaleidoscope is just wondrous because nothing in it changes.

It is merely the turn and the reflection. So your time frames, the situations at birth, a family member, a friend, parent to child, sibling to sibling, sibling to grandfather, it is all connected. You have all been through many lives together simply changing your positions.

This means that in another life time, my mother could be my daughter. My father could be my brother, my grandmother could be a close lifetime friend that lives down the street, or in Agnes' case, she and her mother could be born as twin sisters. The people don't change, it's the positions and the roles that they play during that particular life that changes.

GREG: So then what is the reason to keep on coming? Is it to just learn the lessons?

MA-RYAH: *Yes, to ultimately enter in full remembrance of all you have created before and also to create in absolute love.*

Imagine that you create and you have a life where you enter as child and the parents that you come to, you are conscious that you have come together time after time after time.

You are aware of the moments that you create and you build on love and so each one upholds and supports division of each one to be seen and experienced without any judgment, without any anger. Only love and celebration in enjoyment of one another.

GREG: And we just go through lives together like a bundle of grapes. Like actors, we're all in the same play but each time we perform we each play a different role in the cast.

MA-RYAH: *Yes, very much like that.*

GREG: Well then let me ask you about my son. We have a fantastic relationship. We instantly connected as father and son twelve years ago. We are very much alike. There was always an instant bond. Is there a past connection? Is he in my cluster of grapes?

MA-RYAH: *Oh yes, very much so. It is very seldom that you will have a child which is not a soul that you have created with before. Anytime that you do have one that you have not created with before, it is a choice that is made from spirit side in order to undo similar creations.*

Anytime that you feel very strong closeness with another human you are able to know for certainty that you have knowledge of one another.

When you have someone that you do not connect with at all then you know here is someone that you have not known before and is an opportunity to begin to nourish and to build.

GREG: Okay.

MA-RYAH: *...So then...to transform with your son Joseph, you know each other in Italy. You know each other in Spain. He is your father in France and Japan–very stern father.*

He is also your mother in what is seen as Greece in the 1500 time frame. He is funny then. Your son is funny.

You are also what would be seen as indigenous people in this country together in what is the early 1100 time frame. You are also together as tribal beings in South Africa. You are brothers and he gets you into a lot of trouble. And yet what you came together to fulfill in that time frame was fulfilled. He saves your life from lion.

And what you now know as Holland he is your sister, you are brother but mostly your connection to each other is sibling, a couple times child.

This is the first time you are parent and he is the child, and he does not always like that. Sometimes he wants to reverse that and he becomes acting like parent and seeks to be seen as the parent rather than the child. And it takes gentle reminders that wait, I'm the father and you can watch when you do that because he bristles a bit because he has been parent every other time. So it is beneficial for him to be child to you this time.

It is worth noting that when Joey was two years old, people commented to me that he was an old soul. I remember him at times somewhat acting like an old man. He would say things like, "All done here," and would complain that his back was tired. He was also very decisive and independent. He wanted to do everything himself. At two and a half years old he became a very good negotiator, and at three years old he was using words like: scrumptious, interesting and actually.

AGNES

GREG: I've been thinking a lot about Agnes. I'm wondering what is going on with her. Did she decide to go with her mother to be born as twin sisters? Has she left? No one came up into my room, or at least I didn't hear or see anything. What is happening?

MA-RYAH: *Agnes has...Agnes has not desired to move on. She has decided to stay with you.*

GREG: She's going to stay?

MA-RYAH: *Yes. She put a lot of thought into it and we also spent time there in your house with her. She has not desired to move on to be born with her mother.*

You may have been aware of our presence from time to time. We were spending a lot of time with Agnes to help her to see the energy that she sees and knows as Agnes is still able to be experience with simultaneous of course time. That she is still able to move forward and re-enter. And...she's not wanting to leave you. You are son to her, for her it is like pulling mother from son.

Agnes also knows that when you are 28 years old, she makes commitment to be with you and she has made a commitment to stay with you until transition. She will be one that you will be very aware of when you return to spirit.

GREG: Thank you Agnes! I have to say, I'm very happy to hear it...so what do I do? What do I say to that?

MA-RYAH: *You just thank her for helping you.*

SARAH

GREG: Is Sarah still leaving? What has she decided?

MA-RYAH: *Sarah is getting ready to go.*

GREG: She's definitely going?

MA-RYAH: *Yes she is.*

GREG: How soon?

MA-RYAH: *About eight months your time.*

GREG: So Sarah is going to be born as a baby somewhere. Is she looking forward to having another life?

MA-RYAH: *Yes...she Is a little nervous also, because of how much your world already is impacting her.*

GREG: What do you mean? How is the world impacting her?

MA-RYAH: *As the energy is shifting from spirit to flesh, the veils get thinner so there is more interacting between the dimensions. Sarah is having difficult time right now because your world is having an impact on her...she feels it. So just like a human when you are hit, you feel it. Sarah is beginning to feel it when you pass through her.*

GREG: And this is what happens as spirits get ready to re-enter the earth? They begin to feel the impact of human beings much more?

MA-RYAH: *Yes. Sarah asks us if we will spend some time with her, and we will take her away for a little bit. So she will have like um...refresher course to know how to not receive so much of impact of your world. You will not notice her for a couple weeks of your time.*

GREG: Where is she right now?

MA-RYAH: *She is part way down the stairs...so we are telling her that we will do that with her. We'll take her to our world for a while.*

GREG: Will you bring her back?

MA-RYAH: *Yes, she will return for a while...just taking a little rest from your world.*

Because she has identified so much with being here like child for you, she tells us she has to get her belongings. She wants to get her things. (Long pause) ...So we get ready...we have Sarah get ready.

So we tell her, is alright, you gather your belongings while we pull back thought and we will pick her up.

GREG: I'm going to miss knowing that she is around.

MA-RYAH: *...And for her, Sarah is very sad... scared...very sad.*

I never had a daughter. I have a wonderful son but as I get older I often think of what it would be like to have a daughter and to be a father to a daughter. It's not something I wanted much when I was younger, but now as I get older, I desire to have it more and more.

I very much wanted to see Sarah and at least have that vision in my head of seeing her before she went. She was the one that was around me when I would sleep. She would touch me on my face or on my hand. She showed us her doll on that Thanksgiving night, and she considered herself a daughter to me...such a sweet delightful child. I will always carry around with me the fond memories of four year old Sarah Taylor from the 1920's.

YOU WILL KNOW HER

MA-RYAH: *There is something else...there is something you need to have knowledge of...about Sarah.*

GREG: What?

MA-RYAH: *It is when Sarah comes into this world...*

GREG: Yes, what is it?

MA-RYAH: *When Sarah comes into your world, you will have great awareness of her.*

GREG: I will have great awareness of her? What do you mean?

MA-RYAH: *You are going to know her as human.*

GREG: What? I'm going to know her?

MA-RYAH: *Yes, You will meet her. You will have very strong recognition. You will know that it is Sarah.*

GREG: How will this happen? Is it through a family member? A friend? Will she be a student of mine? How old will she be? How old will I be? When can I expect this?

MA-RYAH: *You will know her from infant.*

GREG: I'm going to meet her as a baby?

MA-RYAH: *Yes.*

GREG: This means that she's going to be born somewhere around here?

MA-RYAH: *Yes.*

GREG: Can you tell me how this is going to happen?

MA-RYAH: *You are going to meet woman. This woman that you are going to meet is going to have a baby. You are not the father of this woman's baby, but you two become friends. The baby that she has is Sarah. This woman that you will meet...her name...has the energy of Stacy.*

GREG: Do I know this woman already? Are we friends now?

MA-RYAH: *No, you have not met this woman yet.*

GREG: Is there anything else?

MA-RYAH: *You will befriend mother. She comes into your life and it is not through your school or through work. It is through your books, when you are selling books and this woman crosses your path.*

She is already slight with child and there is the passing of bodies and as the bodies pass the energies connect and there is, you turn and then she turns, so the eyes, you see each other. And it is not so much a relationship of the heart, joining as partners and such, but more of a relationship of knowing very deeply of one another. In height, she will come up to your heart.

GREG: And she and I will become friends?

MA-RYAH: *Yes, very good friends.*

GREG: Will the relationship last a while?

MA-RYAH: *The rest of life.*

GREG: ...Is it a love relationship?

MA-RYAH: *You are able to choose it to be but it is not what you two come together specifically for.*

GREG: Once Sarah is born, what would happen if I brought her through my house? Would she remember it?

MA-RYAH: *She will recognize. She is still yet small when she is first in your home. So at first, she will not yet have awareness of your language to be able to communicate, but as she learns to be able to speak, she will speak of times that she spent here in your house.*

My hope, wish and desire to see Sarah are actually going to come true after all. I will finally get the chance to see the little girl of Sarah Taylor.

Only it is this time, that she will no longer have the name of Sarah Taylor. She will no longer be a four year old girl with buckled shoes and bows in her hair. She will be living in a different body, in a different time frame, and with a different girl's name.

I always had the fantasy of knowing the spirits in my house as human beings and it looks like the one that I knew the least is now going to be the one that I will know the best. She is coming to my world.

It has been said that children and animals are the most psychic beings on earth. So while she is still young and will remember, I will bring her through my house. I will let her sit where she wants to sit and play where she wants to play, and I will pay very close attention to anything she says while visiting me. Will she talk about the house?

I know that the day will come when I will take out the Christmas tree ornament that I bought of the two children in angel wings. I plan to show it to her. I will hold it in my hand and show her the front of it. I will then turn it around and show her the names Jonathan and Sarah written on the back in gold ink.

I plan to watch her eyes and the expression on her face. Will she recognize it?

I suppose my greatest wish is to have her eyes widen with excitement because she knows that she has seen it before.

And then maybe, when she is a little older, and can communicate in sentences, I will ask her if she can remember any of the things that I said, on that day in December, when I stood in the living room so foolishly holding up the angel winged ornament while talking to the bottom of an empty staircase.

(1) The actual Somers Point home from which the books, *A Father, A Son and A House Full of Ghosts* originated from and were written.

(2) The spot where three funerals were held in the 1930's. The caskets would be laid out all night with the bodies in them. Mimicking sultry woman sat next to me on couch.

(3) The kitchen – where the spirit of Agnes spends most of her time. Hanging on wall is kitchen clock that stops and starts, never keeping the right time.

(4) A view of the upstairs landing taken from the staircase.
Jonathan was standing to the right of the table when I first
learned of him.

(5) Candy dish on the Victrola. The brown furniture is the
Victrola. Notice the picture of my grandmother.
Behind her hanging on wall is her father, "Elbarto" –
A magician who played in Vaudeville.

(6) Three rag dolls for Sarah. Sarah can play with the dolls without physically touching them.

(7) The matchbox cars, plastic soldiers, cowboys and horses that ten year old Jonathan moves on the upstairs landing.

(8) Taken from the living room looking into the dining room and entrance way to kitchen. Danni was standing in kitchen doorway. Big man with vest and watch sits in chair in far right corner of picture, while women sit around table.

(9) Steps leading down to the basement. While holding on to
the railing, ex-wife fell down these steps.
One wonders whether she was pushed.

(10) Inside the kitchen. Agnes was behind me as I sat on the
stool facing the direction of the camera. She was wearing
a blue dress and was to the right of the old red chimney.
Hanging on wall is the Sauvignon Blanc sign that Danni will
tilt from time to time.

(11) The dining room window in which the horrific smell of vomit lasted for close to a year. It was the scent of a dark spirit lurking about, enjoying the turmoil that was happening in the house at the time.

(12) The winged back yellow chair that Sharon will sit in to bring Ma-Ryah through. From this chair, Ma-Ryah has full view of house which includes: living room, dining room, part of kitchen, and stairs leading up to second floor.

(13) The father and son standing on outside deck in front of
main entrance way leading into porch of house.

(14) Side and back view of house.
Back door leads into kitchen.
Both Agnes and Jonathan have spent time out in the yard.

AFTERWARDS

WHAT'S YOUR STORY?

One thing that I learned during this process is that many people have their own ghost stories–something that they couldn't explain and have experienced. They have something to share and maybe never felt comfortable telling anyone. Out of the fear of being judged, ridiculed or laughed at, they decided to keep whatever happened to themselves.

The following stories were told to me by people who had something to say. Some were reluctant to tell them, and some were excited to tell them.

The one thing that they all had in common though, is that they all very much believed in the stories they were telling me.

TERRI – The 1800's

"I just have a very strong connection to the 1800's. I don't know. I just feel like I lived in that time period. I've always enjoyed cross stitching, I'm very interested in learning how to quilt, my favorite books are books on life in the 1800's, and for me, specifically, I feel very connected to the Northeast, the Boston area.

In fact, when I went to visit Louisa May Alcott's house in Concord Massachusetts, I felt such a strong connection that I became emotional."

JUDITH – "It was really strange, my father died two years ago, and while driving in my car the other day I started thinking about him and how I miss him. Suddenly out of nowhere I began to smell his scent."

JOHN – "The old house that I used to rent always had something strange going on. The upstairs, it sounded like a cocktail party. I would always hear glasses clanging together. It was definitely a party atmosphere and it would be right upstairs. There was definitely something going on up there. I heard it a lot."

KATHY – "I went to a psychic the other day and she told me that my deceased grandmother was happy and surrounded by chickens. The psychic told me that if I ever find feathers around my house, that it's my grandmother leaving them. The very next day I picked up the phone to make a call and on the receiver was a feather."

SUE – "You know it's really strange. My daughter has this imaginary friend. She has had this friend since she was 18 months. The friend's name is Zsa Zsa. According to my daughter, Zsa Zsa sits on the end of the bed, plays with her in the bedroom and sits next to her in the car. At one point, my daughter yelled at me to not move the car because Zsa Zsa didn't have her seat belt on."

MARTHA – "About three years ago my mother passed away. Right after that my sister had a miscarriage. Days after that occurred my sister's five year old son said to his mother that his grandmom had come into his room and sat on his bed. She told him that everything was going to be okay."

LYNN – "My dad always used to write me letters and send me articles about teaching. I always loved getting them from him. But I would read them and then I would throw them away. After he died I was very upset that I didn't have them anymore.

Well, it was two years later, after he had died when my husband and I were moving furniture away from the walls because we were getting ready to paint. As we moved the big desk, a strange envelope had fallen to the floor. The envelope was postmarked two years ago and was unopened.

We were a little embarrassed thinking how that could have happened, but the letter happened to be from my father. He must have sent the letter just before he died. It had to have been there for two years. In the letter he told me that he missed me and loved me. I found it on my birthday."

DIANA – "My son David, I remember when he was two years old, he would sit in the high chair and talk to the lamp. He would laugh and talk baby talk to it. He was always talking and laughing to the lamp. It was a one way conversation.

Then when he was somewhere between three and four years old he would say to us, 'That lady came to see me again last night.' Every once in a while he would just come out with this. I would ask, 'Why is the lady coming to see you?'

'Because,' he would say. 'She wants to see her grandson.'

I also remember when he was three years old...he knew...he swore he had lived in Florida. We used to tell him, 'You never lived in Florida. You've lived in New Jersey since you were born.'

Then one day while doing the dishes, I was shocked when he said, 'Do you remember when we lived in Florida in that white house and that little plane crashed in the backyard?'

That had never been discussed anywhere. I didn't even know about it, but when my husband was growing up, he had lived in Florida. And while he lived there a small plane had crashed in the backyard of their white house."

GREG – "I remember I was working as a night watchman a few nights a week at the Flanders hotel in Ocean City. The building had been vacant for months. I was just hired to act as security for a short period of time.

It was around 11:00 o'clock at night towards the end of my shift. I was sitting at a desk in the main lobby watching Tv. when all of a sudden the elevator door opened. Out of nowhere it just opened...but there was nobody in the building and there was no one there.

Elevators don't operate by themselves. Somebody would have had to push those buttons."

TARA – "My uncle died; he lived in Florida. After he had died, my aunt decided she would start taking walks. As it so happens, while she would take her walks, she would always find coins in the middle of the sidewalk.

Later it became a family joke that whenever someone would find a coin while we were visiting Uncle Henry's house in Florida, we would say, 'Oh, it's Uncle Henry saying hi.'

What's strange is, on our last visit, just as I was stepping into the shower, I noticed that there was a quarter in the middle of the bathtub. I know it wasn't there when my children took their showers right before me.

That same day, when I told my husband about the quarter in the middle of the tub, he then told me that earlier that day, that he had discovered three quarters stacked up neatly on the hinge on the back of the bathroom door when he went to take his shower."

DEBBIE – "Seventeen years ago I was on the road going out to dinner with my son when suddenly, I don't know why, I stopped the car and told him we have to go home. I turned the car around and we went home.

When I got home the phone rang. It was the emergency room in Georgia. My mother who was visiting Georgia at the time had been in a car accident. And so within two hours I was on a plane to Georgia.

But that feeling to turn back, I'll never forget it. It was so strong. It was like someone turned the wheel of my car."

LUISA – "I remember taking a fourth grade class on a field trip to the Physick Estate – the old mid 1800's Victorian mansion in Cape May. When I walked into a room on the second floor, I noticed that the rocking chair was rocking. I was the first person in the room. We were the first group. There is no way anyone could have touched it or knocked into it. It was really strange."

JUDITH – "My father was in the hospital dying of cancer. At this particular time he had also developed a terrible fever. At one point, we didn't think he was going to make it. He was barely talking. His fever was so high and he had a massive infection in his arm, he was in really bad shape.

And then there was this woman who came to the hospital room door. She was not dressed as a nurse, had no badge or identification and she just stood at the door with her bright red hair looking in. She never entered the room.

And my father, as bad as shape that he was in and barely able to speak sat up right in his bed and said, 'Oh hi! How are you? It is so good to see you.'

My sisters and I thought that it was oddly strange because it was an exceptionally warm greeting, and for our father...he was so sick and could barely move.

The woman then said something to my father. She said, 'I'm here if you need me.' And then she left. We never saw that woman at the hospital again.

Later, at my father's funeral, we were looking through some old pictures, and a woman who strongly resembled the bright red haired woman who stood at the doorway of my father's hospital room was in one of the pictures. The woman as it turns out, was my fathers sister. She had been dead for 60 years."

GRETA – "My mother recently told me that when she would be home alone, she used to see the outline of a woman in the foyer which led down the hall to the bedroom. She also heard a lot of giggling in the dining room.

She never told me about it until after I moved out. She knew I would get freaked out by it. My mom didn't tell me much after that."

LILLI – "We had a ghost living in the attic above my clothing store. I always heard footsteps and a door shut. I just used to call him, 'Harry.' There was definitely something up there. I would tell this story to people and they thought I was nuts...but I heard it all the time.

My husband would go up in the attic with a flashlight but there was never anything up there. One time we heard what sounded like a chair being dragged across the floor. I sent my husband up to investigate and there was nothing up there, not even a chair.

The one thing that blows our mind is we would always find change in our register when we knew we had no change in there. I just always called him, 'Harry the ghost."

JANET – "I remember when my grandmother was dying of cancer, she had gotten to the point where she was sleeping most of the time. But while she would be sleeping she would be talking and laughing in her sleep. She was talking to friends and relatives and she was calling out their names.

But with every name that she had called out or mentioned, whether friend or relative, they were all deceased. They were all dead. I would stay home so I could hear what she would say next. I was enjoying seeing her laugh."

JANE, ABIGAIL, ALEC – "The first day we moved into the house...oh my god, I could smell it. It was horrible. It was like the smell of urine...throw up. I'll never forget walking in the door and noticing it coming from the staircase. The smell just hit me so strong.

And we had come through this house before to look at it to rent it. I know that there was no smell when we came through it before. And then that first day that we moved in...it was just sickening. It was just as you begin to walk up the staircase, it would hit you. The whole stairway was very intense. But when you got to the kids rooms, there was nothing."

"Yea, at this time there was a lot of stress going on because we were just moving into the house. It wasn't really a happy place. Everyone was kind of over worked and we were yelling at each other. And also I was dealing with problems at school, and fighting, and it wasn't good. Alec tried to ignore it but..."

"That smell was gross. I remember coming home from soccer one day and my mom was on the steps scrubbing the walls and the floor."

"We painted it twice, two coats! We painted the entire hallway up throughout the stairs and nothing could get rid of it. Like Abigail said, at that time we had a lot of things going on. It was not a happy house. Whatever it was, I just feel like it was feeding on the negative that was happening among us.

We're much happier now though. We're moving into our new house soon, and you know it's funny, I haven't smelled it now for a good month."

TERRI – "The music boxes in my house, they're starting to play on their own. It lasts maybe 15-20 seconds, but they've been sitting there untouched for a long time and now they just 'go off.' I'm all alone and I start looking around saying to myself, 'this is weird.' I mean... it's scary.

They were my mother's and she had them all over the house. They're just playing on their own. I wonder if my mom passing away has anything to do with it."

TEACHER – "One of the boys in the class was telling a story about how he had been upset the night before because he couldn't fall asleep. His mom promised to come check up on him and she never did. He had told the class that he was really scared.

Just then one of the girls in the class interrupted and made the point that she's never scared and that she sees people all the time. 'My house is full of people,' she said. 'I see them at night and I see them in day. My house can get very crowded. They are very nice. I can't tell my mom 'cause she would get mad at me."

STEVE, JUDY – "Twenty-three years ago my mother died. She had lingered in the hospital and had been in a coma the last three days, so her death was not a surprise to us.

The hospital had called around 9:00 that night to tell us that she had passed. In fact, the hospital called each of my two sisters also. They asked each of us to come to view her body and to make some arrangements.

Fifteen minutes after receiving that call from the hospital, the phone rang again. It was a very strange phone call. There was static on the other end along with the sound of a week voice with no discernable words. I listened but then hung up after a bit.

It wasn't until four months later, around Christmas when my sisters and I got together. The subject of Mom came up and I mentioned to them the strange call that I had gotten on the night that she died, right after the hospital had called.

As it turns out, each of my sisters also received that same strange call all within the same fifteen minute period.

ANISSA – "My grandmother died before my youngest daughter was born. And Lindsay is three now...but there are certain things that she says and does. When I look at my daughter, I see my grandmother. It's the little things. And when I look at her eyes...there is something in her eyes. It's weird but I definitely think that there is a part of my grandmother in my daughter."

MARIA – "My husband's stepfather died from a stroke when he was around 60 years old. He had a weak heart in addition to that, but it was the stroke that killed him. His name was Bob and this was my father-in-law.

Well, my husband Jay kept having this reoccurring dream. He was having the same dream all of the time. And the dream was that Bob, (his stepfather) was trying to tell him something. He's trying to warn him about something. I remember my husband saying to me, 'I'm hearing him but the words aren't making sense. I can't understand what he is saying. I just know that he is trying to warn me of something. He's trying to tell me something.'

It was a little over nine months later when Jay had a massive heart attack and died. He was 27 years old.

KATHY – "A few weeks ago my son's godmother Jean died. She was a friend. I had known her my entire life. The strange thing is, we were getting ready to clean out her house when one of her coworkers had a strange vivid dream. Now this coworker had never been in Jean's house before but in this vivid dream that she had, Jean took her by the hand and said, 'You have to find the sewing basket. It's small, it has a quilted top with diamond patterns in the quilting. You have to find it.'

Now this dream happened just days before we were about to clean out the house, and a lot of stuff would have been thrown out.

So Melissa, the coworker, clearly remembering this dream, went into the house and searched. She finally found the sewing basket upstairs in the bedroom. It looked exactly as it appeared in the dream. It was small, it had a quilted top and had diamond patterns in the quilting.

She opened it and on the top layer were the usual sewing notions, but when she lifted up the top layer, underneath was filled with old pictures and letters from deceased family members from the past. There wasn't really anything that could hold a dollar value to anyone but it was much more of sentimental value of letters and pictures which dated way back into the family history. Jean did not want this thrown out."

DOLORES – "My mother died a sudden death in 1974. She was 53 years old. And I believe now that part of my granddaughter is my mother.

I have a picture of my mother when she was three years old and next to it I have a picture of my granddaughter when she was almost two. The resemblance is uncanny. In addition to them looking alike, they each have the same natural part and same wave at the exact same spot in their hair. It's weird. Even their fingers are curled in the same position. She just looks like my mother.

Then when my granddaughter was able to talk...she had never been to Philadelphia. She came into our house in Philadelphia where we had all grown up, she sat back in the love seat and said, 'I'm home!'

My sister and I then took her upstairs to see the doll baby. We took her to our mother and father's old room which was now my sister's room. And my sister said, 'Over there Julia, on the bed is the doll baby.' And Julia said, "no...bed there!' She was pointing to where our mom and dad had always kept their bed. Then she laid down on the floor in the same spot where my mother always slept.

We finally got her up and went downstairs and she was playing. It was then we noticed she was in the kitchen on her hands and knees washing the kitchen floor just like our mom used to do. She had a dish rag in her hand and was backing out of the kitchen with the rag in her hands making sure not to step on the part that she had just washed.

Later we showed her a picture of my mother. Now Julia was only 18 months old and had never seen my mother. 'Do you know who this is?' I asked.

'Yes, it's mommy,' she said.

'No, that's not mommy,' I responded.

But then she pointed to a second person in the background of the picture which was my mother's mother.

My sister and I never noticed our grandmother in that picture before.

Later I found a picture of my dad's 65th birthday party. It was a picture of my dad with his brother and two sisters. I said to Julia, 'Do you know who this is?'

'Yes,' she said. She was pointing to my uncle, which was my dad's brother.

'Who's that?' I asked her. 'Who are you pointing to?'

My sister and I were shocked when she said what she said, for she had never heard the name before. She yelled out, 'Hank!'

THE SEEDS OF SHADOW

Fears and Phobias
Remnants of Past Lives

One of our jobs as humans while living these lives is to transform the seeds of shadow; to overcome the negative that we may have experienced in a past life. They may not show up in all of your lives but you are afraid of something and you don't know why. What happened? For the few people below, something happened and it has resurfaced in this life.

DEBBIE – Fear of Title Waves

"I was around ten years old when I started dreaming of title waves. I would dream that I was drowning. It happened night after night and it lasted for years.

When it was time for me to go to college, those dreams determined where I went to college. It had such an impact on me that I built my college plans around it. I ended up going to a college far away from the ocean and way up on a mountain.

Today, it doesn't run my life but whenever I walk the beach, I always check to make sure the water line is where it belongs."

CHRISTOPHER – Jewelry

"I don't like to wear any jewelry whatsoever. Nothing on my wrists, nothing on my fingers and nothing around my neck. I have never worn a watch, a chain; even a wedding ring is difficult for me. Except for clothes, I don't like to wear anything on my body at all...never have.

Just for curiosity sake, I went to a psychic. She told me that in a past life I was a slave and spent most of my life in handcuffs. So having nothing on my body today represents freedom."

SABINA–Fear of Snakes

"I freak out when someone even says the word snake to me. It makes me very uneasy, very anxious. I get very upset.

The only experience I ever had was when I was six years old. I was walking through the backyard and I saw a little garden snake. I remember running back inside the house and I wouldn't come out for days.

I don't know where this fear came from. You can't even joke around with me about snakes. You can't even tell me there is a snake anywhere. I feel violated. We never had one in our house. We never had one as a pet. I just have this terrible fear of them."

STACY – Fear of Matches

"I've lived my whole life with the fear of matches, ever since I could remember as a child. I can't stand what they look like or the smell they give off. Even if it's a single match or a pack of matches, I never want to see them. I've literally gotten sick from the sight of them.

Just the other day I went into my car and my husband had accidentally left a pack of matches sitting on the seat. I had to get away from the car. I went into the house. I mean...it's serious!

When I was younger people would make fun of me and they would do things on purpose but I never thought it was funny. For me, even telling you this story is difficult because I hate even thinking about them.

For me today, people that know me and know about my fear are considerate enough to never have any kind of matches around if I go over their house. They will use a lighter instead if they want to smoke. It's matches...they just bother me so much and I don't know why or where this came from."

JUDITH – Packed Luggage

"When I was six, I became obsessed with the idea that my house was going to catch on fire. I spent a lot of time collecting paper bags, and without telling anyone, a little bit each day, I would take everything I owned and put it into those bags. That included clothing, shoes, even my dresses were shoved in those bags.

And then I would lie awake at night and I would plan how I was going to save those bags. Then I would get up and practice opening up the window, making sure I could open it up fast enough.

Today, forty years later, whatever piece of luggage I own, it has to be very close to me. They are never put away out of sight. And these bags could easily go inside of one another but I'm not able to do that. And some of them...I admit...are packed. They are ready to go. I'm very prepared.

The only difference between now and when I was six is that I no longer practice opening up the window."

FLASHBACK

Summer 2005
Meeting (The Vessel) Sharon

I knew that I had never seen her before. I've lived here for five years but have never seen this woman. I've had many conversations with Lou Ann over these years but I never knew that she had a sister.

The first time I saw her she was standing on the back deck of Lou Ann's house. I was watching from my kitchen window which overlooks the backyards of my property and Lou Ann's property.

I tied up the trash bag and went out the backdoor towards the alley. I dumped the trash in the can and then started back toward the house. While passing the birdbath, I noticed it was dry and decided to fill it.

Lou Ann's sister had her back to me the entire time. She was about seventy-five feet away standing in one spot on Lou Ann's deck. I looked up at her once or twice, but just went about my business.

I was just about to go back inside when I heard a call from across the yard.

"How's your ghost?" She asked me.

"Oh...okay I guess," I called back to her.

She then started to walk closer to where I was standing.

"Lou Ann said that you thought you had something going on," she said with a smile on her face.

"Yeah, I'm pretty sure I do," I said shyly...

APRIL 2007

Two Years Later

GREG: Ma-Ryah, that day, I want to ask you about that day. This was the very first day that I met Sharon in the yard.

MA-RYAH: *Yes.*

GREG: It just seemed so odd that we would meet. It was just around the time when I had strange things going on in my house and it's almost like she was sent to me to help me with it all.

MA-RYAH: *Yes.*

GREG: So I have to ask you...were our paths supposed to cross? Was that supposed to happen? Were she and I supposed to meet each other?

MA-RYAH*: Yes, you were.*

GREG: Why?

MA-RYAH: *Because spirit wants human beings to know that they are loved and cared for...and you are writer. We knew you would write about us.*

Send Questions or Comments To:
gygregory@aol.com

For Other Books by Gregory Young Visit:
www.Jettybooks.com

For More Information About Ma-Ryah Visit:
www.Ma-Ryah.com